SICILY

to explore and to remember

the origins, monuments, museums and sea of this marvellous island

DIACOM4EDIZIONI

DIACOM 4 Edizioni di Salvatore Quattrocchi
Via B. Mattarella, 20 Bagheria 90011 Tel. e Fax 091909141
e-mail: diacom4@virgilio.it

Project by Salvatore Quattrocchi
Texts by Valeria Randazzo
Translation of the text: Tatiana Terranova (to page 111), Margherita Balistreri (from page 112)
Videopaging and cover by Salvatore Quattrocchi

First Edition
Printed on May 2004

Printed by Officine Grafiche Riunite - Palermo

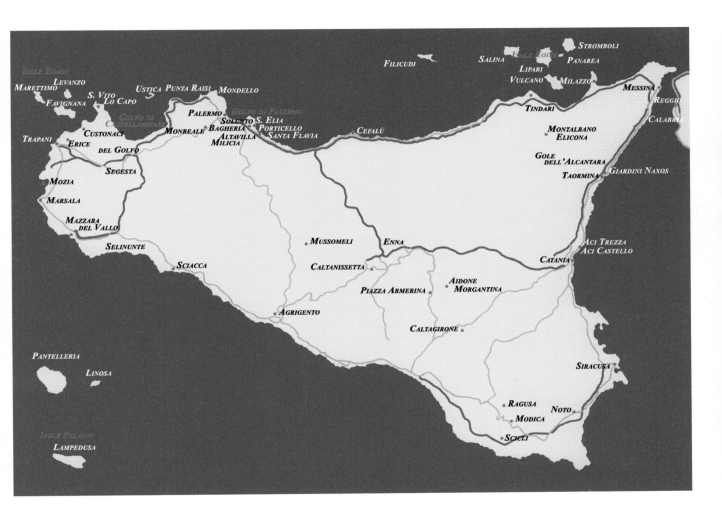

SICILY

Historical hints

Sicily is the biggest island of the Mediterranean and is surrounded by the Eolie, Egadi, Pelagie, Ustica e Pantelleria islands. Sicily is crossed by three mountain ranges the Peloritani, Nebrodi and the Madonias and has the major volcanic apparatus of Europe: the Etna.

Since favoured for its Mediterranean climate, the island has submitted to the colonization of various populations like the Sicani, Elimi, Ausoni and Siculi to the Greeks which arrived in the VIII century b.C. and on its coasts founded the cities Syracuse, Taormina, Agrigento, Selinunte, Imera, Sulunto etc. of which remain numerous testimonies.

Fought for by the Carthaginians against which also intervened Pirro, King of Epiro, Sicily was conquered subsequently also by the Romans. Reduced to province, it became one of the most tranquil and prosperous regions governed by Rome. In the hands of vandals, in the V century a.C, in 535 Sicily was conquered by the Byzantine general Belisario, who gave way to the Byzantine domination under which the conditions of the island worsened. In 827, with the landing at Marsala, started the Muslim conquest of the island which lived great prosperity for about two and a half centuries. In 1060 the Normans landed in Sicily commanded by Roger Altavilla, brother of Roberto il Giuscardo.

In 1130 the kingdom of Sicily was proclaimed and Roger II of Altavilla was crowned first king. Henceforth Sicily entered the Norman kingdom and also with the predecessors Guglielmo I and Guglielmo II the island flourished. During the domination of Fredrick II , the city of Palermo became capital of the State. The most splendid and intellectually the most enriched court of Europe was created.

The crisis started after the death of Fredrick II, with the reign of Manfredi who fell at Benevento in 1250. Carl I of Angiò settled in the kingdom as conqueror and treated Sicily as a province to be punished. The consequence being the insurrection of the Vespers in 1282 and the catching the Angioni from the island.

In 1302, after twenty years of war, Fredrick of Aragona, son of Pietro III, was made king of Sicily under the condition he entitle himself king of Trinacria and that at his death he returned the island to the Angioini of Napoli. The restitution never took place: In fact for the entire XIV century the Aragonesi and Angioini fought for dominance of the island which, in 1412 tied its fait to the Aragonese kingdom and became viceroy. Sicily lived new splendour with Alfonso the Magnificent, who in 1442 reigned also over Naples. Unified Aragon and Castiglia by Ferdinand the Catholic, it was ruled by the Spaniards until11713. Involved in the dynastic wars of the XVIII century, it passed from Vittorio Amadeo II of Savoia to Carlo IV of Austria and lastly to Carlo of Bourbon in 1734, remaining under this last dynasty until 1860. With the Treaty of Vienna in 1815, Sicily became a region of the reign of the two Sicilies: this procured mal content and violent separatist acts like those in 1820, 1831 and 1848. The revolution which exploded in 1860 gave way to Garibaldi to free Sicily with the expedition of the "Mille". The Bourbon reign fallen, the island became part of Italy with a plebiscite in October 1860. From the 15th of May 1946 Sicily is a Region with a special Statute.

PALERMO

Historical hints

Antique and beautiful, Palermo, "Heart of Sicily", has an intense and old history. The greeks called her "Panormo", that is all port, for the geographic position. In fact, provided with a port, defined by Diodoro Siculo the "most beautiful of Sicily", it was connected to Carthago, with whom it maintained tight commercial and political ties. Enclosed between two water ways, the Kemonia and the Papireto, the first nucleus was born between the VIII and the VII century b.C., maintaining its primitive urban order until the Muslim conquest in the IX century a.C., when the city transformed into a Muslim government. With the Norman denomination in 1072, Palermo lived years of great splendor becoming an independent state. During the reign of Frederick II Palermo enjoyed great European prestige especially because it was the cradle to the school of Sicilian poetry, which enticed learned men, scientists, literates, jurists, poets and rhymesters. The vulgar Sicilian was elevated to national language. Since the death of Fredrick II in 1250 until about 1400, Palermo was theatre of political wars and economic downfall. After the revolt of the Vespers in 1282, came the dominations of great noble families such as the Chiaramonte rule. The Chiaramonte presence made the city shine architecturally and was enriched by particular sculptures and decorations of great prestige. Tied to the Aragonese reign, between XV and the XVI century, Palermo had a new political situation and ulterior development. Palazzo Abatellis, Palazzo Ajutamicristo and many others, are the manifestation of the gothic-Catalan style, which is diffused in the Palermitan structures thanks to the famous Sicilian architect Matteo Carnalivari.

The city became the capital of the Spanish viceroy when, in 1516, the crown was passed to Carl V. In sixteen hundred, the affirmation of the Baroque made Palermo outwardly splendid. For a brief period under Saboudo reign, between 1713 and 1718, Palermo returned to Carl III of Bourbon, King of Naples and of Sicily and in 1759 to the son Ferdinand IV. Sculptures, marbles and stuccos enormously enriched buildings, churches and gardens. Sculptors such as Marabitti and stuccoists such as Serpotta, produces and enriched the city with their magnificent works.

After the Congress of Vienna in 1816, Ferdinand with the abolition of the constitution, established an absolutist dominion which provoked the revolutionary movements in 1820. The movements thereafter in 1848 and 1860 saw, for the first time, the population as active part in the revolutions. For many years the city was in complete abandon and site of numerous ruins caused by the Garibaldi battles of 1860, year during which a rebuilding and an intense development started. After the unification of Italy, Palermo enlarged notably and grew also in population. The two World Wars where responsible for the grave damage to the artistic and historical patrimony of the city, which only with a plan of reconstruction in 1947, was able to rebuild. Today, may interventions of restoration have brought the main part of the city to its antique splendour.

PALERMO - CATTEDRALE MARIA SS. ASSUNTA

Was founded by the Archbishop of Palermo Gualtiero Offamilio between 1170 and 1190 but was thereafter enlarged and embellished by the different dominations which where to follow in the course of the centuries. The different periods of construction have, in fact, given origin to the mixture of styles. Prestigious the southern portal, work of Antonio Gambara in 1426, with the wooden door made in 1432 by Francesco Miranda. The inside, shaped as a Latin cross, preserves the graves of the Norman sove-

reigns, the sacred spoils of Santa Rosalia, important frescos and sculptures by very important artists such as Serpotta, Gagini, Pennino, Guercio, Quattrocchi, Velasquez, Novelli etc.. To note the solar meridian, projected at the start of the XIX century by Giuseppe Piazzi; made with a hole in a cupola, at noon enters the light that illuminates the zodiacal sign of the month in a copper rod in the pavement. The treasure of the cathedral is of notable worth, it conserves the golden tiara of Constance of Aragona, found in her grave and decorated with precious gems, enamels and pearls.

PALERMO - CATHEDRAL
HOLY WATER CONTAINER
BY DOMENICO GAGINI

Notable is the Holy water container realized by Domenico Gagini in the XV century.

Placed in front of the column, near the entrance of the southern portal, it shows the angel of Annunciation on its little cupola, while in the shell, the carvings represent the "Benediction of the Baptismal spring" and the "Baptism of Jesus".

PALERMO - CATHEDRAL
CHAPEL OF THE RELICS

In the right aisle (next page) the Chapel of the Relics, it protects the urn of San Mamiliano, Bishop of Palermo in the V century, as well as those of Santa Cristina and of Santa Ninfa, the protectors of Palermo and the relic of Saint Agata's arm. The chapel is enclosed by an iron fence built by Francesco Paolo Palazzotto in 1908.

Palazzo Reale - Sala Pompeiana

PALERMO
REGAL OR NORMAN PALACE

The Palazzo Reale, created as a Punic Roman fortress was reconstructed by the Arabs in the X century and elegantly refined by the Normans in 1072. It was the residence of King Roger II and thereafter of Fredrick II. From the death of Fredrick II in 1250, started the progressive abandonment of the building until the Spanish viceroy, from the XVI century, chose it as their prime abode. The palace, between 1798 and 1806, accommodated Ferdinando di Bourbon as well, who had fled from Naples.

From the four towers that formed the original royal apartments, the Chirimbi and the Greca do not exist any longer while, the Gioaria and the Pisana where lowered for security reasons during 1500.

Inside, there are numerous magnificent rooms such as the "Room of King Roger", "Treasure Room", "Yellow", "Red", "Hercules's", "the Presidents' room", the room for the "Viceroys", the "Chinese" and the "Pompeian" room.

Since 1946, the Palace is the residence of the Regional Sicilian Assembly.

PALERMO - CAPPELLA PALATINA

Found on the inside of the Royal Palace it is a triumph of mosaics and precious marbles. The date of construction is between 1130 and 1132. Originally the left wing was used as private chapel of the royal family, who assisted to the religious functions from the box. The mosaic decorations of the cupola, which represent the Pentecostal Christ, is fruit of able Byzantine creation; the floor is covered with splendid mosaics and geometric motives. In the photo below, the great Fathers of the oriental Church are represented: San Gregorio, San Basilio and San Giovanni Crisostomo.

PALERMO
CAPPELLA PALATINA

In the Cupola, (Photo next page), is one of the most important mosaics of the Chapel.

Designed under the reign of Roger II, it was created by able Byzantine artists.

In the central apse (photo to right), the Pentecostal Christ is represented to the right and at the bottom, the Madonna and on the sides the Saints: Maddalena, Pietro, Giovanni Battista and Giacomo.

"Kars-el-Aziz", that is, wonderful, is the Arab etymon from which the castle gets its name built by Guglielmo I and finished by the son between 1154 and 1160. The building is rectangular and developed on three floors. At the heart of the ground floor is the "Sala della Fontana" characterized by a splendid mosaic décor along the walls.

PALERMO - TEATRO POLITEAMA GARIBALDI

The architect G. Damiani Almeyda designed the theater and was inaugurated in 1874. The style is neo-classic but inspired by Pompeian architecture , shows a curved form at the center of which a triumphant arch, surmounted by a carving of the sculptor B. Civiletti. In the upper part a grand chariot in bronze, opera of Mario Rutelli, and at its side two geniuses on horseback.

PALERMO
TEATRO MASSIMO

The construction of the grand theater in neoclassic style was started in
1875, designed by G.B. Basile but
finished by the son Ernesto in 1897.
The Teatro Massimo is considered
third in Europe after the Paris Opera
and the Opernhaus of Vienna. The
façade is proceeded by an important
staircase to the sides of which are
placed two bronze lions mounted by
figures that represent the Tragedy, by
the sculptor B. Civiletti and Lyrics by
Mario Rutelli. Inside there are five
orders of boxes, most sumptuous
the Royal Box.

PALERMO
PALAZZO ABATELLIS

Today it is the location of the Regional Sicilian Gallery and Archeology Museum. A complete gallery exposes works by Sicilian artists active between the XIV and XVIII century. The museum preserves the works of extraordinary artistic value from the Greek and Roman period and hence considered on of the most important in Italy. The building of Francesco Abatellis was designed and built between 1490 and 1495 in Gothic-Catalan style by Matteo Carnalivari.

PALERMO
PALAZZO ABATELLIS
"L'ANNUNZIATA"

It is one of the most beautiful canvases painted by Antonello of Messina in 1473 and in custody at the Sicilian Regional Gallery at Palazzo Abatellis.

The contrasting colors and the face highlighted by the cape that surrounds it, are very particular.

PALERMO - PALAZZO ABATELLIS - BUST OF ELEONORA OF ARAGONA

Inside the National Gallery of Palazzo Abatellis the famous "Bust of Eleonora of Aragona" is kept. The piece was created around 1468 by the Dalmation sculptor of Zara, Francesco Laurana who worked in Sicily for a few years. The bust represents Spagna Eleonora's infant.

PALERMO
SANTA ROSALIA

The Triumphant chariot of Rosalia represents the most important and most felt religious tradition for the city of Palermo. The 15th oh July, the chariot crosses part of the city bringing the Sacred Images of the Miraculous Patron, whose bones were found in the cave of Monte Pellegrino on the 15th of July 1624. The finding of the relics corresponds with the ending of the plague in the city and the miracle was attributed to the Saint. Since then, every year, S. Rosalia is celebrated with great honors by the city of Palermo.

PALERMO - CHIESA DI SAN GIOVANNI DEGLI EREMITI

The church, a typical example of Norman art, was constructed on the foundations of a VI century Gregorian Convent and partly surrounds the remains of an Arab mosque. It was built by will of Roger II in 1136.
The building appears stocky and square and is surmounted by two red cupolas of Islamic inspiration (Cuban). Inside there is only one aisle, very bare but the little cloister is very suggestive.

ΡΟΓΕΡΙΟΣ ΡΗΞ · ΙC

**PALERMO
CHURCH OF THE
MARTORANA
"KING ROGER II
CROWNED BY CHRIST"**

The mosaic of the Maria SS. of
the Ammiraglio or of Martorana
church, represent Jesus who
crowns Roger II King of Sicily.
The coronation of the King
took place in 1130, by will of the
antipope Anacleto II and the
title was recognized by Pope
Innocenzo II in 1139.

PALERMO
CHURCH OF THE
MARTORANA "GIORGIO
ANTIOCHENA
AT THE FEET OF THE
VIRGIN"

The church of the Martorana was built a bit prior to 1143, year of its completion, by will of Giorgio of Antiochia, the great Admiral of King Roger II.
The mosaic represents him bowed at the feet of the Virgin.

One of the most beautiful piazzas of Palermo it is named after the Pretorio Palace; in this building, built in 1463, the meetings of the Palermitan Senate took place. Today, the Communal Administration of the city resides there. The piazza, of great presence, is decorated, at the center, by a sumptuous fountain, built by the Florentine sculptor Francesco Camilliani, who constructed it between 1554 and 1555. Various statuesque groups all around the fountain, represent pagan divinities, mythological allegories, heads of animals and cherubs. At the shoulders of the piazza rises the S. Giuseppe dei Teatini church, with a cupola covered in majolica policrome. It was designed by the Teatino, Giacomo Besio in 1612 and completed in 1645.

PALERMO - PALAZZINA CINESE

The palace was built in 1799 by will of Ferdinand III of Bourbon using the design of Venanzio Marvuglia. It is in neoclassic style but characterized by Chinese motives. Of particular interest are the frescos and the "mathematical table", ingenious tool created to bring food up and down from the kitchen to the dining room. It was also the preferred residence of Ferdinand IV of Bourbon who hosted the Admiral Orazio Nelson there.

Giacomo Vaccaro's Terracotta group

The museum founded by Giuseppe Pitrè in 1909 is considered one of the most important in Europe and contains a wide collection of objects witnessing the usages and customs of the Sicilian people. The museum lies in the part of "Palazzina Cinese" which was used by Ferdinand III of Borbone and his wife Carolina's servants.

The Sicilian tradition is reconstructed through some objects used for the thread such as spindles and distaffes, ceramics, hunting, sheep-farming and agriculture tools, women and men's week and Sunday customs, wedding and baby's outfits, religious objects

among which handcarts, votive offerings and magical objects, musical instruments and puppets can be found. Of great interest are the cribs among which the one of 1700 ascribed to Giovanni Matera from Trapani.

XIX century woman's costum

PALERMO - MONDELLO

Mesmerizing and fascinating is the golden beach of Mondello, enclose between Mount Pellegrino and Cape Gallo. Locality rich in trees, Hotels, private villas and fun places. It is ideal for who wants to pass memorable evenings or vacations.

PALERMO - MUSEUM OF THE MARIONETTES

The museum of the Marionettes is in Palermo and was started in 1975 thanks to the passionate work of Antonio Pasqualino who in time collected the largest number of puppets and marionettes from all around the world. Among all the collections existing in the museum, those of the typical Palermitan, Catanese, and Neopolitan puppets are indubitably the most vast collection in existence today. The opera of the puppets in Sicily fundamentally represents the story of Orlando and Rinaldo: the chivalrous legends which derive from the French medieval epic, from the "Chanson de geste" and from the story of King Arthur. The Sicilian puppeteers acted out the story by writing a script but improvising the dialogue during the show. Also stories of bandits, of Saints, dramas and farces were represented. The latter, helped to bring moments of fun after the dramatic representations: "Nofriu e Virticchiu" at Palermo, "Peppennino" at Catania, were the Sicilian comic characters that the spectators enjoyed.

The Museum library is also very rich and complete. It holds around 1200 volumes on Marionettes, puppets, popular tradition and a precious collection of scripts and manuscripts from the end of the XIX century and beginning of the XX. Also interesting is the collection of tapes which contain numerous registrations of theatrical shows from different places.

PALERMITAN PUPPETS OF ANGELO CANINO'S THEATER (PHOTO)

This group of puppets is among the oldest that the museum has and belongs to the theater of Angelo Canino, puppeteer from Alcamo, and prior, to the theater of don Liberto Canino; the pieces are dated back to the XIX century.

At the center Carinda stands out, the first puppet with a metallic armor constructed by Don Liberto Canino in 1830; then all around are, the beautiful Angelica, dames, warriors, the King Salatiello, the Christian warriors, the Duke Namo of Bavaria and above, two angels; the one to the right belongs to the Palermitan theater of Vincenzo Argento and is dated 1910-1920.

MONREALE

Historical hints

Those who visit this small Norman city can not help but notice that every nook speaks of history, art and culture.

Magnificent and full of monuments, Monreale is surrounded by a rich vegetation. Its whole story rotates around the construction of the "Duomo". It is said, in fact, that while Guglielmo II, called "the good one", last of the great Norman Kings of Sicily (1153-1189), was hunting in his park and overtaking by fatigue, fell asleep. In his dream appeared a gentle woman who indicated a place in which the treasures of the father were hidden. When he found them, in thanking the woman, who according to the emperor represented the Madonna, had the temple built in that spot. The work started in 1172 and the "Duomo" was dedicated to the Madonna Assunta.

Cathedral - External Apse

MONREALE - CATHEDRAL

One of the most representative Sicilian medieval operas of art is without doubt the "Duomo of Monreale". An authentic architectural jewel in which melt together different styles and cultures such as the Arabian Byzantine and Roman styles. The building was constructed in 1174 on expressed desire of the Norman Guglielmo II. The main view is of a beautiful bronzed portal created in 1186 by Bonanno Pisano, flanked by two square majestic towers. The portal is subdivided into 42 squares in which scenes from the Sacred Scriptures are sculpted. The portal is proceeded by a portico from the XVI century constructed by the Ganginis, separated into three arcades by Doric style columns. The interior has three aisles divided by nine granite columns and one in "cipollino"; the pavement in the area of the altar, marble arranged in a mosaic, dates to the Norman era, while the pavement of the aisles is dated 1500.

MONREALE - CATHEDRAL "PANTOCRATOR CHRIST"

The magnificence of the Monreale Duomo is revealed inside; precious mosaics, with pieces mounted in gold, created between the XII and the XIII century by local artists and Byzantine people, cover the walls of the aisles. In the major apse the image of the Pantocrator Christ stands out in all its splendor. The figure represents Christ in the act of blessing. In the left hand he holds the opened Gospel in Latin: "I am the light of the world. Who follows me will not walk in the darkness". Next to the head of Christ, in Greek letters, the inscription "Pantocrator Christ". The head is crowned by a halo in shape of a cross, symbol of passion. Below Christ, the Madonna with Child between two archangels the apostles.

MONREALE - CATHEDRAL - DECORATIVE WALL MOSAICS

All the walls of the Duomo di Monreale are covered by mosaics which represent the stories of the two Testaments, the creation of Adam, to Christ on a thrown who blesses the world. On the left wall of the central aisle we find the "original sin". Adam and Eve are corrupted by the serpent and are reprimanded by God who bans them from Paradise. Underneath the "sacrifice of Isaac" is represented and "The trip of Rebecca and of the servant Adam", who mounted on two camels are directed to the house of Isaac, son of Abraham, who will become Rebecca's groom.

MONREALE CATHEDRAL BENEDICTINE CLOISTER

Built at the same time as the Cathedral by the will of Guglielmo II, the Cloister represents one of the most beautiful architectural jewels and Roman sculpture that exists in Sicily. The Cloister was built and given in custody to the Benedictines. The Cloister, perfectly square, holds two hundred twenty eight little binary columns, decorated by mosaics, one different from the other and crafted in bas-relief. The capitals are engraved with biblical motives as well as birds and animals that fight and also other scenes.

**MONREALE
CATHEDRAL
BENEDICTINE CLOISTER**

The alternation of the smooth and decorated columns which sustain the very masterfully carved capitals is suggestive and precious.

USTICA

Historical hints

Is one of the most uncontaminated islands in the Mediterranean and is considered a real paradise for skin-divers because it has an extraordinarily clean sea which holds one of the most varying and intact marine flora and fauna. Its sea is so rich and perfect that since 1986 it became the Italian Marine Reserve. It extends for about 16 thousand acres and is locally managed.

It is also the locality of the International Exposition of Skin-diver Activity founded in 1959 and today reached its 42nd edition.

Ustica is located 36 miles north of Palermo and its shape is vaguely similar to a turtle with a surface of about 8 Kilometers. A very small island, it is the emerging part of a volcano dormant since the beginning of the Neozoic age. Its origins lead back to the bronze age, as is seen in the prehistoric village found near some cliffs. The small populated area is in the shape of an amphitheater which envelopes the bay where the port is found. The Tower of Santa

Maria dominates one part of the village and holds the Archeological Museum.

Seen from above, Ustica shows its many colors from a brownish red of the soil, to the black of the lava, the green orchards and fields and the intense blue of the sky and the sea. It is the sea in fact that holds infinite archeological treasures. Its waters are enriched with every type of marine life such as: swordfish, tuna, eels, aluzzi (local barracudas), cernias and saraghi, etc… Its depths are ideal for those fond of submersions; the "Scoglio del Medico" and the "Secca Columbara" are considered an Underwater Archeological Museum" because they preserve numerous examples of Roman jars and anchors of various eras. Between June and September the island hosts conventions, scientific meetings, round tables at which important oceanic experts participate. The thematic photographic contest is also interesting.

AT PAGE 47 SEA BOTTOM

BAGHERIA

Historical hints

In the XVII century, after the news that King Philip IV was dead without leaving an heir, Giuseppe Branciforti began to hope that the predecessor to the throne would be one of his family. But, tired of the plotting by some member of the Palermitan aristocracy and the position consequently taken by the reigning Spanish family, in 1658, the Prince, abandoned Palermo and transferred himself to Bagheria residing in Villa Butera.

It was this residence constructed by Giuseppe Branciforti, Prince of Butera, the starting point for the birth of a new small city. In fact, the Palermitan aristocracy, thanks to Branciforti, discovered the natural beauty of the Bagherese plain with its pleasant climate and closeness to the sea. Villa Palagonia, Villa Cutò and Villa Valguarnera, the oldest, and also Villa Travia, Villa Ingaggiato, Villarosa and Villa Palagonia constructed at the end of the century, were initially places were one spent their holiday. Only on the 21st of September of 1826, with a decree by Ferdinand I and King of the two Sicilies, the preexisting Bagherese community acquired its status as an independent community.

BAGHERIA - VILLA CATTOLICA

Constructed at the entrance of Bagheria between 1706 and 1736 by Francesco Bonanni, Prince of Roccafiorita and Cattolica, it was very visible to all who arrived from Palermo. Imposing and in Baroque style, it has three floors and is proceeded by a hall accessible by means of two symmetrical ramps. Today internally there is an Art Gallery which covets a great part of the Bagherese painter Renato Gottuso's works, whose remains lie in the garden of the villa inside a monument made of Brazilian blue marble.

The splendid Villa Palagonia, also known as the Villa of the Monsters, was built in 1715 by Francesco Ferdinando Gravina, Prince of Palagonia and designed by Tommaso Maria Napoli; in 1749 the villa was bought, as stated in the testament, by the fanciful grandson Franceso Ferdinando Gravina II, who completed its construction and added two hundred monsters made of tufa in the shape of: beggars, satires, deformed midgets, fantastic monsters and characters that had human likenesses, musicians, warriors, etc…, which decorate the entrances and the exterior walls. The main view is of a spectacular double ramped staircase that connects to the nobility floor. The interior has precious decorations be it on the pavement be it on the walls. Splendid and of great effect is the "Hall of Mirrors" whose walls are covered in glass which give the effect of polychromed marble and decorated with medallions carved into the marble by Gagini. In this hall are the busts of Prince of Palagonia, of his ancestors, the Spanish and French rulers. The ceiling is covered by ornate mirrors with images of very colorful birds, fruit and flowers. The other halls are frescoed with mythological scenes.

"Santa Nicolicchia" (Santa Flavia)

SANTA FLAVIA - PORTICELLO - SANT'ELIA

Historical hints

It is a vacation locality most famous for its natural and historical-archeological attractions. Like Bagheria, its development can by dated back to the XVII century with the "phenomenon of the Ville". At the end of 1600 hundred, the Filangeri family built their residence there giving life to Villa Filangeri typically Baroque and around which new constructions concentrated. The population of Santa Flavia began to expand until it became an independent Community after 1860.

Porticello is a small marine fraction of Santa Flavia, visited for its beaches and the "scoglio della formica", favorite place of skin-divers who can admire the very rare black coral there. Another small fraction of Santa Flavia is Sant'Elia, marine area noted for the pureness of the waters and its natural caves.

RUINS OF SOLUNTO

Historical hints

The coming upon of archeological remains along with a series of digs thereafter, bring to light, in 1856, the important populated settlement of Solunto. It was built on Mount Catalfano in the IV century b.C after the conquering and destruction by hand of Dioniso il Vecchio, tyrant of Syracuse, (432-367 b.C.) of a primitive populated settlement of archaic age which had been nearby. The Phoenician name was "Kfr" Kafara, that is village, while the Latin name was "Soluntum" which meant "Rock" and referred itself to the characteristics of the territory. The planning of the city followed the classic Greek urban architectural patterns: the internal streets crossed at straight angles forming ample rectangular isolated blocks.

By means of the "via dell'Agorà" you entered the city. The big street was originally paved with blocks of calcified rocks and moving along it you found yourself in front of many building used for social events. Agorà is, almost like a staircase which brings you to the theater. To the north-east of the theater was a rectangular "Gimnasium". Crossing the via Ippodamo da Mileto you arrive at the splendid "Casa di Leda", named for the fresco found on the inside which represents the "Leggend of Leda", bride to Tindaro. In one of the rooms a mosaic pavement is preserved and thought to be dated back to the II century b.C.

At the entrance of the archeological area there is a small Antique Museum which holds a part of the archeological material from the Solunto digs. Among the remains are the capitals in Doric, Ionic Corinthian styles to that of the middle to late Hellenistic era; some marble statues, a toilet in terracotta for the children in the shape of a shoe, a mill in lava rock, remains of paintings on the wall of Pompeian taste, ceramics, etc.

In the plain of Santa Flavia, at the feet of Solunto, the Necropolis of Solunto" was found. The first tombs were discovered in 1872 near the railway station. One of these contained a rich trousseau of handmade terracotta statuettes from the Hellenistic period and these and more are preserved in the Archeological Museum of Palermo.

SOLUNTO - AGORÀ

Heading down Via Agorà, one arrived at the big piazza, center of public life: the Agorà. Around it were the public structures while the western part was occupied by a large portico called "stoà", of which the row of rooms, the "esedre", carved into the rock, are still preserved.

SOLUNTO - GYMNASIUM

This Gymnasium was reconstructed thanks to the project of Francesco Cavallari in 1866. It was a luxurious private house which was identified as gymnasium due to a Greek inscription dedicated to a gymnast found nearby.

ALTAVILLA MILICIA

Historical hints

The town of Altavilla Milicia is on the Tyrrhenian cost about 24 kilometers from Palermo and is reached using the Palermo-Catania Highway. At the entrance of the town there is the famous Sanctuary of the Madonna of Milicia which attracts thousands of people in pilgrimage each year; the Museum of the Sanctuary holds about 400 small votive paintings which are offered to the Madonna to give thanks for a grace received. In the territory, besides the beautiful sea , (see photo on next page) you will find the remains of historical structures which are dated back to the Normans and Saracens such as the Church of S. Maria of Campogrosso also called "Chiesazza". This church was founded in 1070 by Roberto il Guiscardo, the church was attached to a monastery of "Basiliani" monks. The Saracen Bridge on the S. Michele torrent and the three guard towers, (photo below) were built along the coast as a system of defense from pirate invasions.

CEFALU'

Historical hints

Diodoro Siculo already spoke of Cefali in the IV century b.C., the antique city rich in history and natural beauty. Remains of medieval and Norman Arab structures oppose themselves to the ocean front tourist localities which cover the long golden coast.

The Arabs occupied her in 858 a.C. and in 1063 was conquered by the Normans, whose domination brought the city to economic prosperity and political power. In 1131 the city became one of the most important residences for Bishops and the Duomo, built by Roger II, King of Sicily, demonstrated its magnificence and strength. Reconstructed on the shore of the sea, Cefalù was defended by a powerful town wall interrupted by guard towers. The city lived a period of great urban expansion during the feudal dominion of the Chiaramonte family and in 1348 and thereafter in 1352 by the Ventimiglia family. The importance of Cefalù grew all the more when in May of 1775 it was given the title and the prerogative of Senate. With the administrative reorganization of the reign in 1812, Cefalù was the location for the Subintendance and capital of one of twenty three Sicilian districts. When in 1856 the revolution against the Bourbons started, the city actively participated. Then, in 1860 Garibaldi chose this city as locality for the government committee and for the district committee and gave the presidency to the baron Enrico Piraino of Mandralisca.

Cefalù - Cathedral

It is the most imposing religious structure of Cefalù, built by will of Roger II in 1131. The interior is divided into three aisles by 16 granite columns mounted by roman and Byzantine capitals. Decorated in part by very precious mosaics on a golden background, dated back to 1148, in the basin of the apse the handmade Byzantine "Pentecostal Christ" stands out. The church preserves notable works among which the "Madonna with Child" by Antonello Gagini dated 1533 and a wooden crucifix from the thirteen hundreds painted by Tommaso de Vigilia.

Recent restoration on the ceiling of the transept have brought a wooden table with painted decorations from the "Ruggeriana age", vividly colored with geometric animal and plant shapes.

From the interior of the structure you can access the beautiful Cloister of the Cathedral considered and important example of medieval Sicilian architecture. It was built in 1100 and is square shaped and surrounded by columns with decorated capitals.

Cefalù
Museo Mandralisca
Cratere

Among the archeological finds at the Mandralisca Museum the famous crater of the "Tuna vendor" stands out. It has the shape of a bell and the technique is that of the black bottom with red marks. It comes from Lipari and is of Sicilian manufacturing dated IV century b.C.

CEFALU'
MUSEO MANDRALISCA

Out of all the private museums it is the riches in remains collected and preserved by the Baron Enrico Piraino of Mandralisca. It holds about six thousands volumes, from the 1500 - 1600, among which history texts, literature, philosophy, natural science and new-spapers from eighteen hundred. The coin collection is one of the richest and most complete and includes Greek, Roman and antique Sicilian coins. Some of the coins are rare examples of notable artistic prestige. The pictorial works with paintings, are from various periods from the Byzantine school to the XVIII century: canvases by Ruoppolo, Pietro Novelli, Antonello De Saliba and the famous "portrait of an unknown" by Antonello di Messina, dated 1470. The museum has among others and archeological collection with finds that come from Lipari such as an antique crater from the V century. Also found; masks, lamps, little vases, clay objects, perfume burners, all of which dated back to the III and II century b.C.. The mollusk collection is particular and includes numerous species of Mediterranean sea shells and examples of terrestrial Sicilian Mollusks. To complete the collection, there are the fossils of shells dated back to the Neozoic age which come from the Palermitan area.

CEFALU'
MUSEO MANDRALISCA
RITRATTO DI IGNOTO DI
ANTONELLO DA MESSINA

Besides all the various pictorial works, the most famous in custody at the Madralisca Museum is the "Portrait of an Unknown" by Antonello di Messina. Dated to 1465-70, it is one of the main works of the Sicilian painter known also for the "Annunziata" kept at the Regional Gallery of the Abatellis Palace in Palermo.

Cefalù - Public Wash Basins

The public wash basins are one of the most particular corners of Cefalù. It is carved in rock and has medieval origins.

MONTALBANO ELICONA

Historical hints

A small medieval suburb situated in the Nebrodi mountains at an altitude of 907 meters, Montalbano Elicona is full of suggestive and marvelous natural sceneries. Already in the second half of the XII century a.C., the geographer Edrisi mentioned

A MEGALITH
REPRESENTING A
PRAYING

A MEGALITH
REPRESENTING A
DEMON

Montalbano in his "Book about King Roger" revealing the presence of Lombard colonies which originated from different parts of Italy. Fredrick II of Swabia gave it as dowry to his wife Costanza of Altaville and being an important strategic point, he strengthened the fortifications. In 1233 the Lombard colonies present in Sicily, rebelled against the Emperor after the promulgation of the Melfi Constitutions, inducing the destruction of Montalbano and to deport the population to Augusta and to Palermo. Montalbano, returns to its antique splendor. and became the "Regia Aedes" of the emperor Fredrick II of Aragona, who between the end of 1200 hundreds and the beginning of 1300 hundreds, made the castle even more secure with the construction of a new wall. Having become a fief and thereafter a duchy, it was sold by the Princes of Cattolica to the Company of Jesus and after having been property of the State, it was transformed into a Commune. There is a lot of interest in the megalithic area of Montalbano and is a goal for students and tourists. The area developed around the Argimosco site and beyond Mount Castellazzo, is marked by the presence of the Menhir, Dolmen and Tholos, called "Cubburi". According to some scholars, it seems that the "cubburi" where designated for funeral purposes, while others believed they were used as habitations.

MONTALBANO ELICONA - CASTLE

The majestic Swabian-Aragonese Castle of Montalbano dated thirteen hundreds, dominates over the antique houses of the medieval suburb from above. Built originally to defend, in the first half of the XIII century was also accessorized by a tower and a wall. In the first years of the thirteen hundreds, Fredrick of Aragona built that which then became the "Regia Aedes" that is the royal summer residence. Today the structure appears in all its splendor and visitors have the incredible sensation of reliving medieval times for a few moments.

MILAZZO

Historical hints

Mythical land of the Sun God, home of the giant "Polifemo" and landing ground of the "mythical" Ulysses, Milazzo was already inhabited in the Neolithic age (around 4000 b.C.). Fought over by different populations between the VIII and the III century b.C. such as the people from Athens, Syracuse, the Mamertini and the Carthaginians. The victory of the Consol Caio Duilio in the battle between Romans and Carthaginians during the Punic wars, in 260 b.C:, established that Rome dominate Mylae, the Greek city of Milazzo, founded in 649 b.C..

Raised to Roman Municipality by Ottaviano Augusto, it was presented with the imperial eagle as its new heraldic stem. Under the dominion of Fredrick II of Swabia, the city became fortified and enjoyed the important privileges until the end of the Spanish domination. In 1295, in Milazzo, there was a Sicilian General Parliament. Thereafter it was also the protagonist of a multitude of conflicts, sieges and conspiracies , until the Napoleonic Wars between 1805 and 1815 and also liberalist and rebellious insurrections of 1821 and 1848. It was also involved in the Garibaldi enterprise of 1860 and in the second world war.

Rich of marvelous beaches and coves, art and history, Milazzo is an ideal place for a wonderful stay and the discovery of a part of eastern Sicily. You can choose excursions to the Castle, the Spanish quarters, the Medieval area to the mesmerizing Eolie Islands and so diving into the past and into the crystal waters of the Tyrrhenian.

ISOLE EOLIE

Historical hints

These Eolie islands emerged during the glacial period and are of volcanic origin and are still subject to eruptions and seismic phenomenon that are responsible for their continuous modifications in dimension and physical aspect. The largest are; Lipari, Vulcano and Salina and the smaller; Stromboli, Panarea, Alicudi and Filicudi and all offer intact landscapes and crystal waters.

Already populated in the last centuries of the V millennium, probably due to the Sicilian men moving there, commerce developed and the working of obsidian, a volcanic glass, which was obtained from the lava flows, was exported in the whole Western Mediterranean for the manufacturing of cutting instruments. The demographic development and the economic well being which was possible due to this commerce, began to decrease with the discovery of using metals. From the XVI century b.C: the relations with the Aegean world were intensified and this is true in Lipari, where there is a presence of various "micenee" ceramic remains found on the island. Between 1430 and 1270 b.C. the Milazzo culture is followed by the culture of Ausonio I and Ausonio II.

The oldest story of Lipàra, that begets its name from Liparo, son of King Ausonio, is characterized by the rivalry and conflicts with the Etruscans who were permanently beaten by Ierone, tyrant of Syracuse, in 474 b.C. in the battle of Cuma. Having become a naval base during the Punic Wars in 269 b.C., it was conquered by the Romans in 252-51 b.C.. After the devastation by the Arabs in 838 a.C., the islands remained uninhabited until the arrival of the Normans who settled in the Castle of the Benedictine Monks. Annexed to the two Sicilies in 1589, they remained under the dominion of the Spanish until Italy unified.

The tourists that arrive to the islands by sailing along the marvelous bays, enjoy the splendid sea which alternates from an intense blue to an emerald green in color. Volcano, still active as is Stromboli, emits from its crater and from openings in the ground, fumes of vapor, sulfur and carbon nitrate at high temperatures. Bathing in these waters gives a pleasant sensation of well being. The volcanic sands are black and fine and contrast with the very white "pumice beaches" of Lipari and the marvelous underwater experience rich in marine pant life , yellow "gorgonie", sponge colonies that offer the sea lover unforgettable sights.

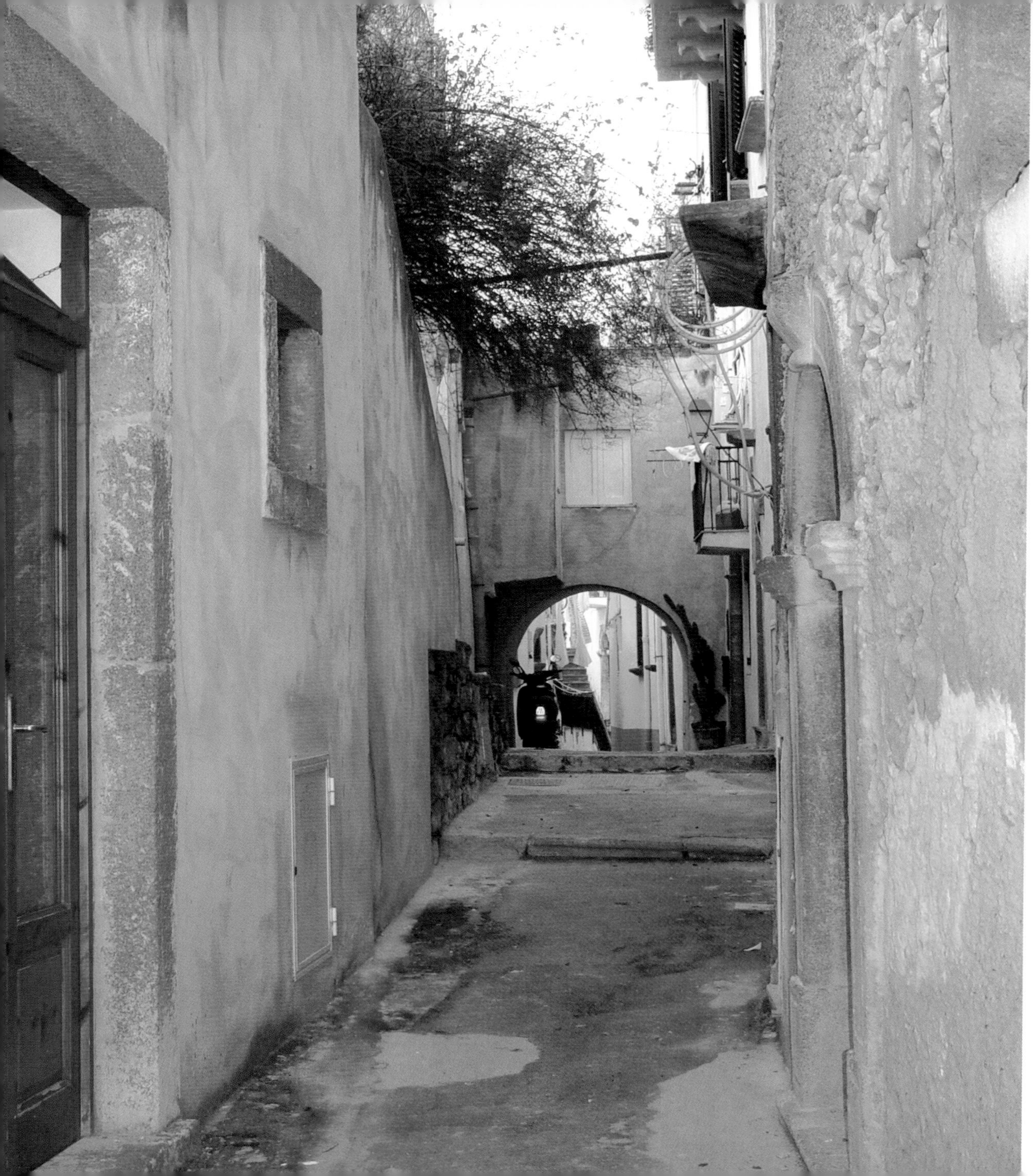

Lipari
Alley

Pag. 75
Lipari
Cave of
the
Angels

TINDARI - SANCTUARY AND REMAINS OF GYMNASIUM OR ROMAN BASILICA

The sanctuary of Tindari, designed by the architect Vincenzo Piccini, saw the first stone placed in 1965. The grandiose structure is embellished by precious frescos, esteemed marbles, beautiful mosaics, inlay and wonderful windows. Internally, behind the altar is the miraculous and "brown" Madonna of Tindari. At a small distance there are the remains of a structure dated back to the first years of Roman conquest but there is a doubt as to whether it is a gymnasium or a Basilica. Recent restorations lead to the thought that the structure was meant for another purpose: for example a Monumental "Propileo" or be it a portico which proceeds the entrance of a temple or royal palace.

MESSINA

Historical hints

It is situated on the north-eastern part of Sicily on the strait from which it gats its name and which separates the island from Calabria. It was founded by the Siculi in the second half of the VIII century b.C. and they called it Zancle, (crescent). Invaded by the Messeni who transformed its name to Messana, in 396 was destroyed by the Carthaginians. After the first Punic War it became Roman and lived a period of great prosperity that continued during the Byzantine, the Saracen and the Norman dominion in 1061. In the XII century during the period of the Crusades, it became one of the most important Mediterranean ports for the trade of silk, wool and leather.

There was another moment of cultural and commercial growth under the Aragonite and thereafter the Spanish dominion; in 1733, Messina passed to the Bourbons. The plague of 1743, which made 40.000 victims, then the earthquake in 1783, brought the city to a great downfall. In 1854 there was the cholera, which killed about 15.000 and the earthquake in 1894 and the followed in 1908 brought the city to its feet. In the years to follow, Messina developed and became a big commercial and tourist center; today the city presents itself as a modern and full of receptive structures.

XVI century.

On the left side of the "Duomo" rises a 60 meter high bell tower, reconstructed on the base of the original, by the Ungerer company of Strasburg. It has a big mechanical clock with four quadrants. On the south side of the tower there are two quadrants with a planetary calendar and with a globe that indicated the lunar phases. It is the biggest automaton clock in the world, which begin to function every twelve hours be it during the day or night. The figures that are represented in the nooks of the bell tower and are connected to the city's history and to its religious tradition. On the top of the steeple a Norman lion on his hind legs, holds the flag with the golden cross, that the Emperor Arcadio gave to the city. Underneath, a golden singing rooster is between Dina and Clarenza, two popular heroines of the Sicilian Vespers war. Then there is the delivering of the Sacred letter to the Virgin by the Messina embassy and the Sanctuary of Montalto, sacred to the war of the Vespers. Every quarter hour rotate the four ages of man that is youth, adolescence, adulthood and the age of senility and finally death. The chariot tied to a buck indicated the passing of the days in the week.

Messina - Duomo

More than once modified and reconstructed, the Duomo was built by Roger II and consecrated in 1197, during the reign of Enrico VI of Swabia; the church was dedicated to the Virgin Maria. The original Gothic-Norman plan was modified in time due to the damages caused by a fire in 1254, an earthquake in 1783 which destroyed the bell tower and the façade, the earthquake in 1908 and finally, during the second world war, by the bombardments in 1943. It was then reconstructed by the archbishop Angelo Paino based on the original plan.

The actual façade is decorated with polichromed marble strips; it preserves three portals in a late-gothic style the major one is flanked by two lions dated to the thirteen hundreds. The high steeple is held up by three columns on which statues of Saints and Angels rest. In the superior steeple, dominates the "Christ crowning the Virgin", dated 1464-77, while in the lunette of the portal the "Madonna with Child" stands out. The latter was sculptured by Mazzolo in 1534. The interior is divided into three aisles by 26 monolithic columns surmounted by original ogive arches and covered by a painted trussed roof . Among the works which avoided destruction is the statue of S. Giovanni Battista attributed to Antonello Gagini and the Chapel of the Sacrament, designed by Jacopo Del Duca, Michelangelo's scholar, in the

In the piazza before the "Duomo" there is the fountain of Orione built by Angelo Montorsi in 1547: it is one of the few sculptural works that survived the various cataclysms. The Fountain, the polygonal basin, celebrates the construction of the first aqueduct of Messina. The human figures at the edges of the fountain represent the Tevere, Nile and Camaro Rivers. A body with tritons and naiads sustains, at the top, the statue of Orion, mythical founder of the city.

MESSINA - CHIESA DEI CATALANI

Built between 1150 and 1200 on the remains of the pagan temple of Neptune, it is an example of different styles based on a late Byzantine architecture. Externally, the chromatic game with the rocks, the blind little loggia and the prolonged plant of the church go back to the Islamic and Byzantine Orient. It was given to the city by Ferdinand the Catholic after having been the royal chapel until 1507. The church, dated to the XVI century, was denominated by the Catalane after awarding the structure to the Catalane merchant's political clique. The church is lower in respect to the rest of the city, which is more elevated due to the reconstruction on remains, after the earthquakes.

GOLE DELL'ALCANTARA

The Gorges of Alcantara, discovered towards the fifties, are still today partly unexplored due to the dangerous waters that flow in certain points. It seems that the river bed of Alcantara was formed in prehistoric times following some lava flows. The river is incandescent, in its descent towards the ocean, eroded all that came into its way before flowing into the ocean. After, the lava bed was occupied by the Alcantara River which begins in the Nebrodi Mountains and covers about 48 Kilometers before it flows into the Ionic Sea. Its waters, during the years, smoothed the bed of the river and probably, where the earth was more porous, it dug even more giving life to imposing lava walls of incredible beauty: the Gorges of Alcantara. Full of little waterfalls and artificial lakes, they are usually 5 meters wide and the waters that flow here are 50 meters high in some points.

TAORMINA

Historical hints

Taoromenion was founded by the Siculi on Mount Tauro. The same place, already populated in the Archaic age by the inhabitants of the close by Zancle (Messina) and by the same Siculi. It welcomed also the inhabitants of Naxos, who settled it after the destruction of their city by Dionigi I (403 b.C.). It became under the guidance of Andromaco, father of the historic Timeo, in 358, city of Greek imprint. It remained under the dominion of Agatocle, tyrant of Syracuse, for about five years, until it was defeated by the Carthaginians at Ecnomo in 310 b.C. and the city was taken by Ierone II of Syracuse. At the death of Agatocle, the Romans conquered the city and renamed it Taoromenium. The city saw a period of great splendor that ended during the servile wars of 135-132 b.C. and the battles between Ottaviano and Pompeo. Dominated by the Byzantines until the end of the IX century, it was completely destroyed in 962 by the Arabs and after having been reconstructed, it was conquered by the Normans of Roger of Altaville in 1079. Under the Norman dominion Taormina became economically and commercially important and enriched itself with numerous works of art.

During the war of the Vesper, in 1282, it remained loyal to the Argons and in 1411 welcomed the Sicilian Parliament for the election of Fredrick, count of Luna, to King of Sicily.

Toarmina participated in the battle against the Bourbons, the lords of the two Sicilies and in 1860, in occasion of Garibaldi's arrival in Sicily, freed itself of them.

Today Taormina is a city rich in tourism due to the culture and natural beauty. Its monuments give us the testimony of the different populations which dominated it. All this is associated to the marvelous view of the sea, the golden beaches, the beautiful bays, caverns, and the enchanting gulf that envelopes "Isola Bella"; in the distance one perceives the imposing Etna in continuous eruption.

TAORMINA - GREEK THEATER

Second to the Theater of Syracuse, its construction dates to the Hellenistic period, during the domination of Gerone I in the II century b.C.. It was thereafter modified by the Romans that adapted it to the performances of gladiators, naval battles (naumachie), hunting performances, etc.... The orchestra was amplified to suit the new performances and pits were caved to host the

combat of the gladiators and wild beasts. The spectator stands, carved out of rock, could hold 5400 spectators; two arcades crowned it and the superior, sustained by columns, hosted the spectators during the intervals of the representations.

ALLEY

TAORMINA - BASILICA CATTEDRALE "SAN NICOLÒ DI BARI"

The cathedral is entitled to "S. Nicolò" and is a structure from the twelve hundreds, reconstructed between the XV and the XVI century. The façade shows rough blocks of stone, the cathedral is enriched by a rose window dated fifteen hundreds and it has an ornate portal dated sixteen hundreds. The interior, divided into three aisles by granite columns, is enriched by interesting works of art, among which a polyptych by Antonello de Saliba and a painting of Antonino Giuffrè of the XV century which represents the "Visitation and the Saints Giuseppe and Zaccaria". Noteworthy is also a sculpture dated fifteen hundreds in alabaster, of "gaginesca" school.

The Piazza del Duomo is embellished by the elegant Fountain built in 1635. At the top, a "two footed centaur", which holds a globe in its hands, became the symbol of the city. The base of the fountain is adorned by mythological figures. All around there are other four smaller fountains on the tops of which is a sea horse.

TAORMINA - BASILICA CATTEDRALE "SAN NICOLÒ DI BARI" - POLYPTYCH BY ANTONELLO DE SALIBA

Precious, at the inside of the Cathedral is the Polyptych on wood by Antonello de Saliba dated 1504, representing the "Virgin with Child, the Saints Girolamo and Sebastiano, the Pietà and the Saints Lucia and Agata".

TAORMINA - PIAZZA IX APRILE

Piazza IX of April represents one of the most suggestive corners of the city. The view moves from the Sanctuary of the Madonna della Rocca, to the slopes of Mount Tauro, the Ionic coastline and then lost in the distance at the top of the smoking Volcano, the Etna. The piazza is characterized by the Tower of the Clock which through the "Porta di Mezzo", introduces the Medieval part of the city. It is a stone structure towered over by blackbirds under which is a big clock. Literally at the tower, the Church of San Giuseppe rises at the height of a double staircase. The Baroque facade has a grand portal while at its side there is an elegant

Bell. The interior is preciously decorated with stuccos from the XVIII century and canvases from the sixteen hundreds.
The view overlooks the whole coast with the bay of the "Giardini Naxos" to "Capo Taormina" and "Capo Schirò". The piazza is also a social place for whom wants to enjoy the marvelous nature and contemporarily, tickle the palate with excellent typical Sicilian sweets, found in numerous places which are in the open, that frame the atmosphere.

Also called Mongibello, from the Arab Gibel Utlamat, it is the most active volcano of Northeastern Sicily. It is also the highest volcano in Europe and one of the biggest in the world. Its height surpasses 3300 meters but changes due to its frequent mutations due to the overlapping of eruptive material. The Etna rises on a very vast area of the Piana of Catania, between the rivers Alcàntara and Simeto. It formed in the glacial era, it has intense periods of activity during which it emits great quantities of lava. Memorable, in fact, the eruption of 1669, whose lava collided with Catania and also destroyed the Etna Volcano Observatory "V.Bellini", which

ETNA

was reconstructed in a different area. The Etna is an interesting tourist attraction at any time of year. Depending on the altitude one reaches, you sense the climactic differences and the change in vegetation. There are areas cultivated with citrus fruits, almonds, olive and fruit trees to woodsy areas of chestnuts, oaks, beech and conifers. Since 1987 a Etna's Natural Regional Park has been institutionalized which extends from the peak to the foot of the mountain. It is possible to make excursions to the craters and to assist to the continuous eruptions, or go to the skiing area reached by taking the lifts which reach 2350 meters of altitude.

ACICASTELLO - ACITREZZA

Historical hints

Acicastello, which starts as a small village of fisherman, is an important tourist spot of international fame, rich of tradition and history.

That which characterizes this town the most is the Norman Castle, constructed on an immense cliff, which emerged after an underwater eruption. The Castle, planned probably in 800 a.C., was an Arab residence for about two centuries; passed to Roger of Lauria, it was conquered by Fredrick II of Aragona in 1297. Today, it is the site of the Civic Museum which preserves holds interesting archeological remains, as well as mineral, animal and vegetation remains.

Acicastello, including its history, its picturesque streets and its lush vegetation preserves a "Myth": it is said , in fact, that the pastor Aci, in love with the sweet nymph Galatea, was killed by a huge rock thrown by "Polifemo", blinded by his jealousy because his love is not corresponded.

The God Neptune, felt pity for the pain struck nymph, transformed the lover into a river which flows towards the sea, home of Galatea, and allows the encounter of the two lovers (hence the name Acicastello).

But Acicastello, has more than 1.000 things to tell among which "the yell of the Cyclopes Polifemo" who by throwing rocks against Ulysses gave origin to the Lachea island and to the "Fariglioni".

Acitrezza, a sub fraction of Acicastello, is the city of Verga, who was inspired by this town to write "I Malavoglia".

Acitrezza was also the picturesque backdrop for the film by Luchino Visconti "La terra trema"(The earth trembles). The famous producer was inspired it seems by the social attention with which the author G. Verga handled the problems of the fishermen in his book.

Acitrezza "Pearl" of the Ionic is very famous because it holds the "Faraglioni and Isola Lachea" in its waters which are today a Protected Marine Area.

Castello Normanno

CATANIA

Historical hints

Founded in 729 b.C. by Greek colonists from Calcide, Katane remained under their dominion for about three centuries. In 476 b.C. it was conquered by Gerone from Syracuse, who chased away the people of Calcide and renamed this city Aitna (Etna). The city recovered its primitive name when the Syracuse tyranny fell in 461 b.C..

Conquered by the Romans in 263, at the beginning of the Punic Wars, Catania confirmed its importance and prestige. The incursions by the Vandals, during the V century a.C., were responsible for notable damage to the city. Of the Arab conquest, in 827, few traces remain. More evident, instead, the negotiation between the emir of Syracuse Ibn al-Werd and the Normans who in 1071 entered Catania, guided by the Great Count Roger. For more than one and a half centuries it was a feudal city until a terrible earthquake in 1169 destroyed everything. Thirty years after the earthquake, the city revolted against Enrico VI and again in 1232 against Frederick II, under which Catania became a royal city and recognized as a Commune.

The fourteen hundreds were a period of great commercial expansion during which the feudal families affirmed themselves. Wounded by the popular tumults of 1647, it was partly destroyed by the eruption of the Etna in 1669; in 1693 a potent earthquake destroyed everything. The seventeen hundreds were utilized for reconstruction of the city while in the eighteen hundreds the city flourished again culturally and economically.

CATANIA - DUOMO DI "SANT'AGATA"

Built by Count Roger and by the Bishop Ansgerio, between 1078 and 1093, on the remains of the Achillian spa, it was destroyed in the earthquake of 1693. Reconstructed, of the original construction, it preserves only three apses, the part of the transept and two lateral donjons. The interior of the structure is constructed with square lava blocks and inside Roman columns are visible that originate from a Roman theater. The Polychrome Baroque frontal view is of two orders of columns. Above it is decorated by the statue of Sant'Agata to whom the Dome is dedicated.

The interior has three aisles divided by pillars and preserves known graves among which we want to remember the grave of Vincenzo Bellini, Costanza d'Aragona, wife of Fredrick III and other royal Aragonites. An ornate marble portal dated 1495 opens into the chapel in which the relics of Sant'Agata and part of her treasure are preserved.

Duomo of "Sant'Agata"

CATANIA - URSINO CASTLE

It was built by Riccardo of Lentini by will of Fredrick II of Swabia between 1239 and 1250. Originally the Castle rose near the sea, from which, following the volcanic eruption in 1669, it was distanced due to the lava that filled in the moat and the bastions. The structure has a square foundation, four angular cylindrical towers and two are laterally semi-cylindrical. In the fourteen hundreds it was the political and residential location of the Aragonites.

Today the castle is site of the Civic Museum and was inaugurated by king Vittorio Emanuele III in 1934. It hosts various collections among which those of the Benedictines, the Baron Zappalà-Asmundo and that of the Prince of Biscari. Among the works that are part of the collection we want to mention the prehistoric Greek and Roman vases; Siceliote and Roman sculpture and coins; mosaics, armor from the XV and XVI centuries, medieval and renaissance sculptures, various paintings, etc.

CATANIA - BELLINIANO MUSEUM

"This house where Vincenzo Bellini was born was declared National Monument on the 29th of November 1923".

Here the musician Vincenzo Bellini was born on November the 3rd 1801 and remained until he was 15, then, after the birth of his brothers, the parents transferred themselves into a bigger home. The father Rosario, organist and composer of sacred music, transmitted the love for music to him and was also his first teacher. Today the house of the "Cigno" (Swan) of Catania has become the Belliniano Museum and preserves objects, paintings and manuscripts that belonged to the musician.

CATANIA - BELLINIANO MUSEUM

The halls of memories hold also the instruments an which Bellini learned to play and compose the operas: "Adelson and Salvini", "Bianca and Fernando", "Il Pirata", "La straniera", "Norma", "I Capuleti and the Montecchi", "La sonnambula", "I Puritani" etc…, that were represented not only in the biggest theaters of Italy but also in London and Paris, where the musician died in 1835.

CATANIA - BELLINIANO MUSEUM

Inside the Belliniano Museum there are various objects that belonged to the musician Vincenzo Bellini. The walls and the show windows expose manuscripts of the musician, various autographs, the funeral mask, portraits, postcards and various trinkets.

The Benedicine Monastery of San Niclolò l'Arena was founded in 1136 and reconstructed after the earthquake of 1693 with Baroque sumptuousness. It is considered the second in Europe for its largeness only behind the Mafra in Portugal and since 1997 hosts the Faculty of Literature of the University of Catania. The second of the cloisters that are part of the monastery, is enriched by a magnificent marble and arched colonnade, designed in 1609 by Giulio Lasso. At the center there was a marble fountain which presently results unassembled.

CATANIA BENEDICTINE MONASTERY
STAIRWELL

Inside the Monastery, The "Stairwell of Honor" conduces to the superior floor. Columns of neoclassic imprint sustain the ramps and the bi-chromic stuccos on the walls represent episodes dealing with Saint Agata, San Benedetto and San Nicolò.

CATANIA - MONASTERO DEI BENEDETTINI - BIBLIOTECA URSINO - RECUPERO "SALA VACCARINI"

The Monastery is also the location of the "Riunite Civica and Ursino Recupero" Libraries, one of the richest cultural citizens institutions, which preserves more than 210.000 volumes and more manuscripts, parchments, miniature codes, incunabula, drawings, newspapers and periodicals.

Vaccarini Hall was thought by the theologist Nicolò M. Riccioli and realized in 1773 by G.B. Vaccarini. It is a true architectural

jewel which extends itself over a surface of 400 sq. meters.
Rich shelving in wood, in which the books are held and a gallery where chairs and shelves alternate, are illuminated by the light that enters through the oval windows. The ceiling is decorated with allegorical pictures by Papiro and the pavement is covered by Neapolitan majolica of the seventeen hundreds.

CATANIA - AMPHITHEATER

Dated to the II century a.C., the amphitheater is found at the center of Piazza Stesicoro. The stairwell, sculpted in the lava rock, with 32 orders of seats, were able to hold about 15000 spectators.

CATANIA - BELLINI THEATER

Constructed in 1890 by Carlo Sada, it was inaugurated on the 31st May 1890 with the "Norma" by Vincenzo Bellini, to whom the theater is entitled. The front view, on the baluster of the façade, is a marble group that stands out and which represents "The winged Victory the crowns the Music and the Poem"; underneath is the bust of Vincenzo Bellini. Splendid is the Hall of the Theater, to which Sada dedicated great care; formed by four orders of boxes, marvelously decorated in gold, it holds up to 1500 spectators. At the center the royal balcony stands out. The ceiling, painted by Ernesto Ballandi, represents "The apotheosis of Bellini".

SYRACUSE

Historical hints

Antique and magnificent city on the eastern coast of Sicily, Syracuse is one of the places that almost completely still shows its glorious past. Syracuse was colonized in 734 b.C by Corinthians, who settled in the Island of Ortigia, establishing one of the most important Western Greek settle-colonies. After almost one century from its foundation, Syracuse had reached such a prosperity as to found other cities in the neighbour countries. In 485 the tyrant Hielon, already tyrant of Gela, stretching his rule on Syracuse and joining forces with Teron, tyrant of Agrigento, succeeded in defeating Carthaginians in the battle Himera. Hielon's successor was his brother Hieron who defeated Etruscans in Cumae in 474. The city, one of the most thriving in the Mediterranean, lived in a democratic system for a short period as far as Dionysius came to the throne (405 - 367). Under Dionysius, Syracuse was a real power: he developed the port, built gymnasium, temples and changed Ortigia in a stronghold and inexpugnable fortress. The following year the last war against Carthage took place, in 367 B.C., Dionysius died, leaving his throne to his son Dionysius II. He, being an inexpert governor, reached an agreement with Carthage. After 24 years of reign, in 343 B.C. Dionysius II left Syracuse. His successors were Timoleon and Agatocles, who took possession of the city through a coup d'état in 316. When Agatocles died, there were again civil wars in the city. Hieron II was the last tyrant to rule Syracuse, giving the city a long period of peace and prosperity, that lasted until the falling of the Romans in 212 A.C. Romans made Syracuse the capital of the Roman province in Sicily; in the V century A.C. Syracuse lived a period of peace until the Vandal's invasion, which caused the end of the Western Roman Empire. The Byzantine Empire had been lasting for three centuries; the city was sacked and this, together with the barbarian invasions, was the start of its slow decline. Syracuse was definitively occupied by the Arabs in 878; in 1091 it passed to the Normans and became Aragon and later Angevin and Habsburg possession. In 1693 Syracuse was destroyed by an earthquake which upset Val di Noto; because of many collapses thousands of people died, and churches, houses and palaces were destroyed. In 1865, thanks to the annexation of Sicily Kingdom to Italy Kingdom, Syracuse became a chief town again and became the seat of the Prefecture. The city expanded on the mainland giving life to new buildings. Today Syracuse, but in particular Ortigia, keeps its ancient aspect that approaches different cultures. The beauty of its natural port and the green of its environs make it one of the most charming cities in antique Sicily.

SYRACUSE - SANTUARIO DELLA MADONNA DELLE LACRIME

Solemn and particular is the Sanctuary of Madonna delle Lacrime, its spire is 94,30 metres high. The Sanctuary of the Madonna delle Lacrime (Our Lady of tears) was built by two French architects, Michel Andrault and Pierre Parat in 1954. The Sanctuary displays the sacred image of the Madonna who began to shed tears on 29 August 1953 and in the following days; on 1st September tears were seen again on the Virgin's face. A commission appointed by the archiepiscopal Curia ascertained the tears to be human. In one of the altars, on the right of high altar, the urn containing the tears of the Miraculous Virgin, visible to the believers, is kept.

MADONNA DELLE LACRIME

SYRACUSE - TOMBA DI ARCHIMEDE

Among the tombs in the Necropolis of Grotticelli, nearby the Archeological Park, two tombs have been obtained from rock, they are decorated with Doric column in relief, sourmonted by a tympanum pediment. One of these tombs is dedicated to Archimedes, physicist, mathematician and astronomer, born in Syracuse in 287 B.C. and famous for several inventions and discoveries in mathematical field. In fact the tomb in the necropolis wouldn't be the Archimedes' tomb, because it is a columbarium, that is a sepulchral room of Roman age. There aren't many tombs with hole of Greek period, but we are certain that Archimedes is buried in the same necropolis.

SYRACUSE - GREEK THEATER

It is one of the greatest theatre in the Greek world and it was built during the Kingdom of Hieron II by Demokopos, maybe between 238 and 215 B.C.. In the theatre of Syracuse, for the first time, Aeschilus played the premiere of Aeschilus's tragedy "The Persians" and, in 476 B.C.,"Etnee", written to celebrate the foundation of Etna by Hieron I the Etnean. The part which is better preserved is dug in the rock while missing the high part of the cavea, whose blocks were used by the Spaniards to built its defensive bastions in the Island of Ortigia. The theatre has undergone a lot of changes, above all in the period of the Romans that suited it for their shows of hunting beasts, circus games, struggles of gladiators and water games.

117

SYRACUSE DUOMO

Magnificient baroque witness, the Cathedral in Syracuse was partly realized on a preexisting Greek Temple, devoted to Athena, of which the ionic columns are still visible. It introduces a façade rich in doric columns that is the frame to the "Virgin" of Ignazio Mirabitti, of 1572. The inside is enriched in several works of art of Antonello and Domenico Gagini, in paintings attributed to Antonello da Messina and painters of the"antonelliana school". The 1658 Baroque altar, attributed to Giovanni Vermexio, has a monolith table of the temple trabeation, collapsed in 1693 because of the earthquake.

SYRACUSE
ORECCHIO DI DIONISIO

It is one of the most interesting archaelogical attractions of the city of Syracuse, and the most famous cave of Latomia del Paradiso. Tuchydides tells about it as a place in which 7000 Athenians were brought as prisoners, between difficulties and deprivations, following the defeat suffered by the Syracusans in the 413 B.C. The name is given by the human form of an ear, through which the tyrant Dionigi, according to the legend, was to listen to the words of the prisoners, thanks to the acoustic feature of the cave.

SYRACUSE
MUSEO ARCHEOLOGICO
REGIONALE "PAOLO ORSI"
"STATUE OF THE VENUS
ANADIOMENE"

The Regional Archaelogical Museum Paolo Orsi has been opened to the public in 1998 in a new site, transferring the already existing dating 1886 in Piazza della Cattedrale. The uninterrupted activity of excavation of the archaeologist Paolo Orsi of Trento, from which the museum takes the name, has enriched the archaeology field showing the uses and the different cultures of the people that have preceded us. The inside of the museum is divided into sectors: around 18000 archaeological manufactured pieces are exposed according to their chronological succession. Among the so many works preserved there is the "Venus Anadiomene", emerging from the sea; it is the most beautiful work in the Museum in Syracuse. It was recovered again in 1804 in Syracuse and it was also said "Venus Landolina" from its discoverer's name . The Statue is a Roman final draft from the original Greek one of the II century b.C.

The sector B of the Archaeological Museum in Syracuse is devoted to the Greek colonies. Some findings originate from the ionic colonies of Naxos (Giardini), Mylai (Milazzo), Katane (Catania) and Leontinoi (Lentini). Much space is devoted to doric colony of Megara Hiblaea, that collects the most ancient materials in ceramics of archaic Greek age and a series of recovered manufactured pieces both in the necropolises of the colony and in the urban air. Remarkable is the painted calcareous sculpture representing the "Mother Goddess" who nurses two twins, "Kourotrophos." The statue dates back to the half of the VI century B.C. and it originates from the necropolis of Megara Hiblaea.

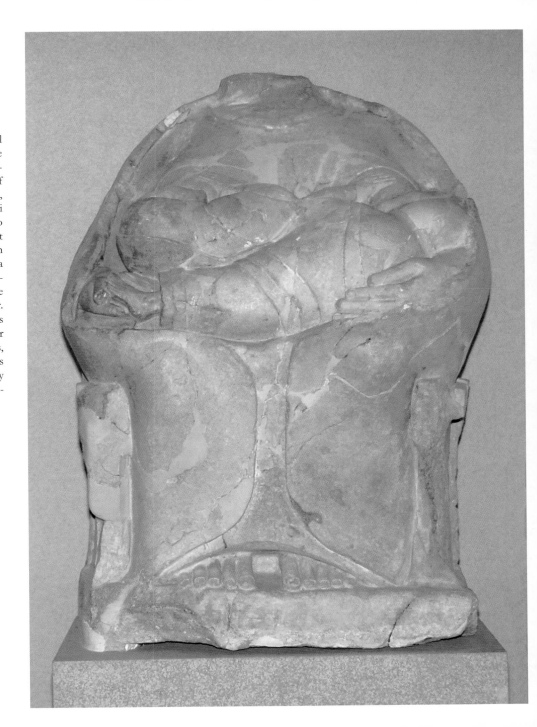

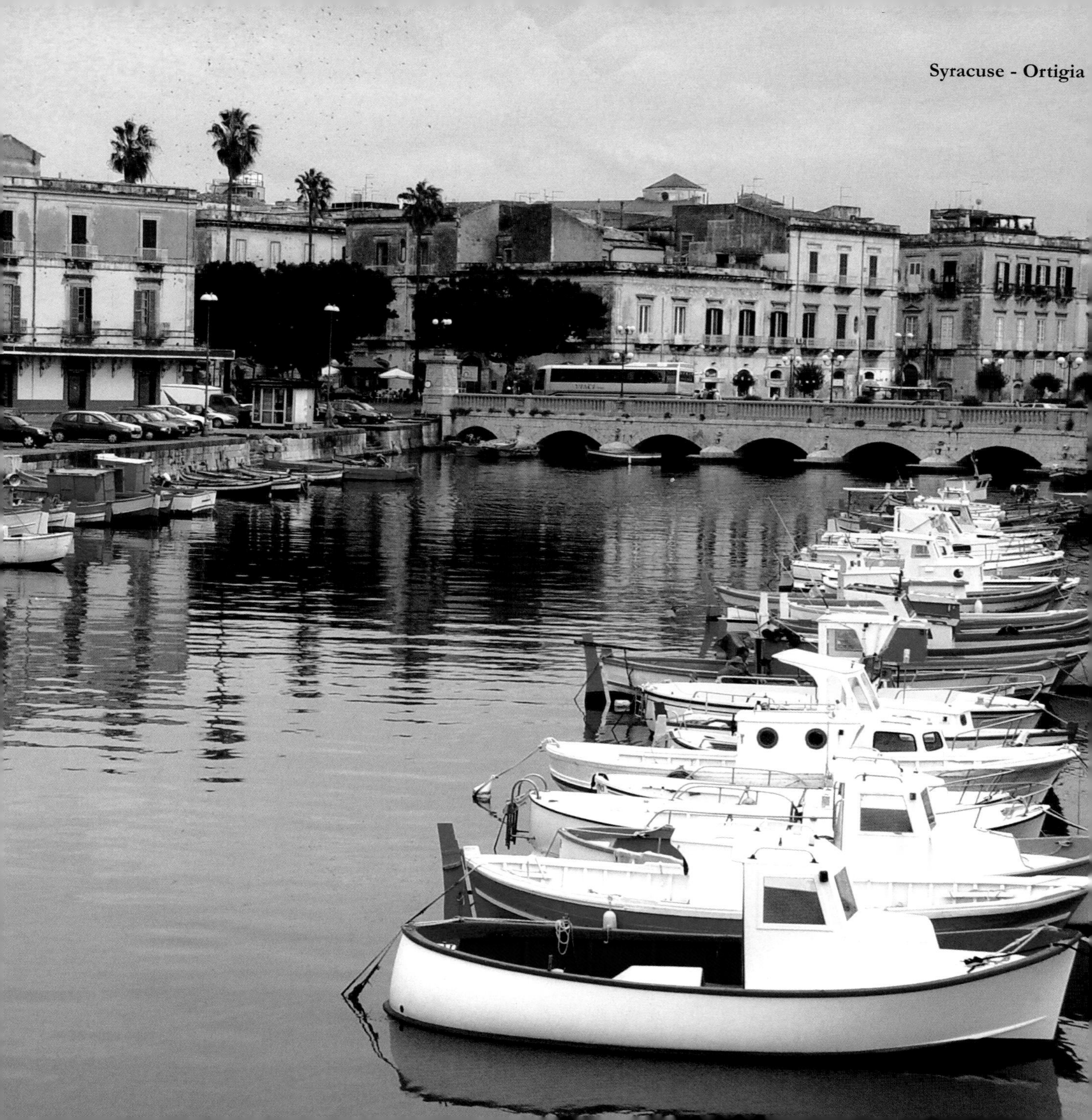

Syracuse - Ortigia

SYRACUSE - TEMPIO DI APOLLO

A Greek inscription, engraved on the tallest step of the frontispiece, attests that the building was devoted to Apollo. The doric temple, considered the most ancient of the Greek West, was raised by Kleomene and Epiklès realized its columns. The temple was built with calcareous stone of Syracuse and it has undergone several transformations during the centuries. In Byzantine period it became a church and later under the Arabs a mosque. It was also inserted in the Spanish Barrack of the Old District, built in 1562. When between 1858 and 1942 the monument was released, the rests of the temple ,even mutilate, were visible to visitors.

SYRACUSE - SAN GIOVANNI ALLE CATACOMBE

The Church of San Giovanni Evangelista, according to the tradition, holds St. Marcano's spoils, first Bishop of Syracuse, martyred under Gallieno and Valeriano in the III century. It was considered the ancient Cathedral in Syracuse for a long period. After the 1693 earthquake, the façade and the portico were reconstructed with the addition of fifteenth-century elements. The inside in three aisles divided by 12 columns in doric style (what they refer to the Apostles), gives access through a staircase, to the Catacombs. Begun in the IV century and widened up to the V, they contain thousand of burial niches and frescos along the walls. A sarcophagus of the late IV century with the representation of biblical and evangelical scenes can be admired.

NOTO

Historical hints

Declared "Capital of the Baroque art" from the Council of Europe, Noto preserves its visible prehistoric origins through the findings recovered in its territory. A lot of graves dug in the calcareous rocks date back to the civilization of the Siculians. In the near regions the civilizations of "Castelluccio" had developed among the XVIII and the XV century B.C., skilled in the ceramics production and "Finocchito" among the VIII and the VII century B.C..

The Greeks, penetrated from Syracuse toward the inside of Sicily, settled Noto in the 450 B.C. and became its dominators. Several witnesses of their domination have come to light: remains of gymnasium, traces of walls and other findings dating back to the III-II century B.C. Undergone by Ierone II, tyrant of Syracuse, it took the name of Netumn and had a period of great development.

It became "civitas foederata" under the dominion of the Romans and it had as privilege the exemption from the tax payment.

Of the Byzantine period few traces have remained after the Arabic conquest in 866; it became chief town of the area of the Val of Noto and the strongest fortress in Sicily. Under the Arabs the city increased its economy, thanks to the cultivation of the citrus fruit and the silk workmanship. Such prosperity grew even more during the Norman and Aragonese domination. It also had the privilege to give birth to famous men as the humanist Giovanni Aurispa, the jurist Andrea Barbazio and the architect Matteo Carnalivari, so that, in 1503, Ferdinando the Catholic conferred it the title of "Urbs ingeniosa." Among the XVI and the XVII century the city became rich in buildings, churches, convents, squares and roads but the disastrous earthquake razed it to the ground in 1693.

The new city was reconstructed in 1703, 8 miles far from the preexisting one, and famous architects worked in this reconstruction; furthermore valid stonecutter succeeded in creating an extraordinary urbanistic center of great artistic value. In fact, today, the "Baroque of Noto" is known in the world for its features and for the wonderful gilded colors which are typical of the sandstone tuff, the stone used for the new constructions. After a long and slow period of economic recovery, Noto started again shining under the Bourbon dynasty. It became "Consulate of commerce", during Charles III's Kingdom but, in 1817 it lost the role of chief town that had been given Syracuse.

What remained of the antique medieval Noto is a heap of ruins hidden by a thick vegetation. The Royal Door of Ancient Noto, the walls and the remains of the castle, witness the preexisting city, dating back to the XVII century B.C. and destroyed by the earthquake in January 11th 1693. Walking through paths we can perceive remains of churches, of buildings, of roads, of the gymnasium, and of the Heroas, which were the veneration places of the dead heroes, witness of the Greek period.

Noto - San Francesco Church

San Francesco Church stands in the summit of a long stairway on Piazza XXX October. It was built in the first decade of 1700 and complieted in 1776 on Rosario Gagliardi and Vincent Sinatra's project. A baroque portal gives access to the church in an only aisle, rich in Gianforma's plasters from Palermo. There are two paintings representing "The ecstasy of S. Francesco" and "S. Antonio that preaches to the fishes" of O. Scozzi. Beside the church the Monastery of the Savior, a monumental complex of great scenographical effect ,was erected.

NOTO - PALAZZO DUCEZIO

In front of the Cathedral, in the great square, Palazzo Ducezio rises. The ancient building was planned by the architect Vincenzo Sinatra, the works started in 1746 and were completed in the following century. The project foresaw the construction of an only floor, in 1951 the second one was also erected.

A semicircular stairway brings to the entry. Inside the representative room of the ground floor there is a fresco in the vault attributed to A. Mazza, representing "King Ducezio that marks the site of ancient Noto."

NOTO - CHIESA DI SAN DOMENICO

The building, Rosario Gagliardo's work, introduces a façade rich in columns and it is considered one of the most remarkable expressions of the Baroque art in Noto. It has a nave and two aisles and contains precious paintings, plasters and a magnificent marmoreal altar-piece with tiles of the Via Crucis. Also a ciborium in gilded wood and in the sacristy a lavabo of the XVII century are preseved. On the left of the church the attached convent shows a magnificent ashlar portal realized by Vincenzo Sinatra.

Noto Palazzo Nicolaci di Villadorata

On the homonym street Palace Nicolaci of Villadorata stands. The realization is to be attributed to Labisi and it is considered one of the most magnificient palaces in the city. The façade is very particular with balconies decorated by satyrs, mythological animals and chimeras. As soon as we go away from the central portal, the sculptures seem to be all of the same size. The inside has sumptuously frescoed rooms and a courtyard in clear stone.

SCICLI

Historical hints

Fascinating town extending on a lowland among the rocky hills of St. Matteo, of the Rosario and of the Cross, Scicli was destroyed from the 1693 earthquake and reconstructed in late Baroque forms. The presence in the site of neolithic settlements and some of the copper age is documented through many archaeological recoveries. Conquered by the Siculians that probably gave it the name, it suffered the dominion of the Greeks and the Romans that made it "decumana city". Between the VII and the VIII centuries A.C. it was the territory of the Byzantines that built the first nucleus of the castle as a defense of the Barbaric raids. The building was widened by the Arabs which conquered Scicli in 864. What we remember of the Norman domination, in particular, the victorious clash with the Saracens,which occured in 1901 in the area of Milici. Later under the Aragonese dominion , the city belonged to the county of Modica. Of the following periods little is known: among the '400 and the '500 quite a lot ecclesiastical institutions and 27 brotherhoods were founded. In 1600 Scicli was forced to suffer various calamities; a pestilence, in 1626, that reduced of two thirds the population; the 1693 catastrophic earthquake that razed it to the ground and finally in 1709, an invasion of locusts that damaged the crops, causing a serious famine. In 1817 the new administrative bourbon model went into effect and the city saw a new economic and social rebirth. Today Scicli, together with other seven cities of south-oriental Sicily, has been inserted in the list of the Unesco and recognized as "World Heritage Site." Such recognition has been ascribed above all to Palazzo Beneventano and Street Mormina Penna on which, in perfect harmony, baroque buildings, rococo, neo-classic and liberty buildings lean out.

SCICLI - CHIESA E CONVENTO DEL CARMINE

Over Piazza Busacca the monumental complex of the church and the convent of the Carmine leans out. The building, typical example of rococo style, was planned by Friar Alberto Maria of St. Giovanni Battista; the oriental façade of the convent, always of the same architect dates back to 1775. The inside in one only nave is decorated in white stuccoes and was realized by Giovanni Gianforma at the beginning of 1700; it is, besides, embellished by the altars in marble of Tommaso Privitera, by precious paintings attributed to Costantino Carasi of Noto and from a "Madonna of the Carmine" in silver of 1760. The Convent of the Carmine is, in the façade, stylistically homogeneous to the Church.

SCICLI - CHIESA DI SAN MATTEO

St. Matteo's church is the old matrix of Scicli. The building of medieval origin was widened during the centuries. Destroyed by 1693 earthquake, it was reconstructed in the '700 with basilical plant with 3 naves and two aisles. In 1874 it was closed to the cult but has remained as dominant symbol of the city.

SCICLI - PALAZZO BENEVENTANO

Considered by the Unesco as "World Heritage Site", Palazzo Beneventano is, perhaps, one of the most characteristic of Sicily of the eighteenth century. Grotesque details embellish the façade of the building whose planner is anonymous: the balconies, from the elaborate form and from the grilles as "breast of goose", are supported by shelves representing fantastic animals. Monstrous and grotesque sculptures, Moors and Saracens' heads and the statue of St. Joseph enrich the building façade.

PALAZZO BENEVENTANO

MODICA

Historical hints

Modica extends on a rocky spur, upon two throats dug by the two streams Ianni Mauro and Pozzo of the Pruni.

The city of Modica has very ancient origins: lived by the Siculians and then by the Greeks, it is quoted by Cicero, during the Roman occupation, when in the "Verrine" he attaches Verre for his oppressions against the Sicilian cities.

The Byzantine necropolises have left the traces of the people of Bisanzio in Modica after the fall of the Roman Empire. In 844-45 it was conquered by the Arabs and it became a big agricultural and commercial center; later around two centuries of Arabic domination, in 1091 it was conquered by the Norman ones. Roger the Norman's children were invested with the title of Earls of Modica and later the city passed first under Angevin and later Aragonese dominion.

Governed by the Chiaramontes for about one century, the city was enriched in architectural works. To the Chiaramontes follo-

wed the Cabreras and so the Henriquezes, who remained to Modica till to 1702. Meanwhile the city had been razed to the ground by the earthquake of 1693 and lost the importance that had had up to that moment. When in 1926 Ragusa became chief town of province, Modica, that during the wars of the Risorgimento had become chief town of one of the three districts that composed the province in Syracuse, had to conform itself to the new social-political situation .

The city, divided in Modica Alta (upper town) and Modica Bassa (lower town) contains a great artistic patrimony. A typically Baroque city, it also was cultural characters' birthplace among which we remember Girolamo Ragusa, historian, poet and philosopher, dead in 1720; the historian Placido Carrafa, the scientist and philosopher Tommaso Campailla (1668-1740) and the poet and literary man Salvatore Quasimodo (1901-1968), Nobel Prize for Literature in 1959.

MODICA - DUOMO DI SAN PIETRO

In Modica Bassa a wide stairway, animated by the statues of the twelve Apostles, gives access to St. Pietro Cathedral. The building with a seventeenth-century features on the first floor, introduces on the second, referable stylistic elements dating back to the half of the eighteenth century with some tendencies to Rococo. The inside, with one nave and two aisles and divided from Corinthian columns, preserves the marble statue of "Madonna of Trapani", dating XV and XVI century and the beautiful marmoreal statue of Benedetto Civiletti, 1893, representing "St. Pietro and the paralytic". There are, besides, a silvery shrine of 1643 and some eighteenth-century paintings. The central nave is frescoed with "Scenes of the New and Old Testament."

MODICA
DUOMO DI SAN GIORGIO

In the highest part of the city and on the summit of an ample stairway, which joins the upper part to the lower one, the Church of St. George, the most monumental construction in Baroque Sicily stately stands.

It was probably built on a preexisting church devoted to the Saint Cross, destroyed in the 845; it was reconstructed in Norman age at the end of the XI century. Damaged by the 1693 earthquake it was reconstructed between the XVIII and the XIX century. The inside preserves arches, valuable plasters, marbles, a silver altar, paintings and a reeds organ in graven and decorated wood in gold. There is a precious painting of Fillippo Paladino, 1610, representing "L'Assunta", a silver urn containing St. George's relics and the wonderful Polipthyc set behind the altar.

MODICA
DUOMO DI SAN GIORGIO
POLITTICO

The whole frontal part of the apsidal vain is covered by a magnificient Polipthyc attributed to Bernardino Niger, dating 1573. The work, composed by nine rectangular tables and by a lunette put on as a crowning, representing the Mystery of the Salvation. In the center God the Father is set; from left to right, the Pentecost, the Resurrection, the Ascension, the Presentation to the Temple, the adoration of the Magis, Jesus among the Doctors, S. Giorgio, the Sacred Family and S. Martino are represented. The wooden frame is very precious.

Ragusa

Historical hints

The city of Ragusa rises among the valleys of the Iblei Mountains and is separated in two parts: the most ancient, Ibla, reconstructed after the 1693 earthquake on the preexisting city and the new one situated in a denominated area called Patro.

The origins of Ragusa are very ancient: it was founded by the Siculians around 3000 years ago, as the graves and the funeral findings discovered in Gonfalone's valley attest, it was occupied by the Greeks who called it Hibla Herea. In the second half of the III century it became, under the Romans, decumana city and it was called Hereusium. The name was still changed into Reusia under Byzantines' dominion, who strengthened the city with powerful walls and built a Castle to defend themselves from the continuous raids of the Barbarians (Vandals, Goths and Visigoths). Conquered by the Arabs, in the 848, the city took the name of Rakkusa or Ragus. It was in Norman age, in 1100, that Ragusa developed and became a county under Goffredo of Altavilla, Roger I's son. Following the Aragonese dominion, it passed to the powerful family of the Chiaramontes that governed it for more than one century. Their successors were the Cabreras, that extended the County but aroused the malcontent of the people of Ragusa that divided it in two factions, causing for centuries civil struggles.

Destroyed by the earthquake, it was rebuilt in two separate sites: Ragusa and Ibla, that were definitely unified in 1926 when the city became chief town of province.

Today Ragusa is a city rich in churches and buildings that embellish it and that make it one of the most beautiful town of the Sicilian Baroque.

RAGUSA - CATTEDRALE DI SAN GIOVANNI

St. Giovanni's Cathedral is the most representative building of Ragusa. Built in 1694 it rises, imposing, on the homonym square. The church is founded on an wide terrace and introduces a rich Baroque façade on two orders. Of the three portals the central one is overhung by a niche containing the statue of the Virgin with her Child, placed side by side by the statues of the Saints Giovanni Evangelista and Giovanni Battista. The inside with a 3 nave and two aisles Latin cross introduces two orders of columns, in typical asphaltic stone of Ragusa, with Corinthian capitals. In the various chapels works of great importance are preserved, among which a painting representing St. Filippo Neri, of Sebastiano Conca; a "Virgin" of Dario Guerci, of XIX century and "St. Gregorio" of Paolo Vetri. The reliquary urn is one of the greatest treasures of the goldsmith's Sicilian art.

Cattedrale di San Giovanni

RAGUSA
CASTELLO DI DONNAFUGATA

The ex feud of Donnafugata, a few kilometers from Ragusa, has very ancient origins. It was a Byzantine settlement up to the conquest of the Arabs and it remained later unused for centuries.

The origin of the name is not certain; probably it refers to the famous "escape" of the vicar of the Kingdom, Bianca Navarra, wife of the King Martino, because of the undesired attentions of the elderly Count of Modica. At his death King Martino had named Giacomo Arezzo and Bianca herself, as regent of the Kingdom of Sicily. Since 1410 the Arezzo family was owner of almost all the neighboring feuds of the castle. In 1845-47, Francesco Arezzo, Baron Conrad's father, began the restauration of a little holiday house, with a courtyard next to an old squared tower. "Sober and elegant carpets to be put back in Donnafugata" were commissioned to Naples and Palermo. Many rooms were widened and, in the saloon of the weapons, all the coats of arms of the families allied in the centuries with the Arezzos were painted. The building, initially as country residence became high middle-class residence at the end of the ninenteenth century. The noble floor was enriched with representative rooms, picture gallery, billiard room , living rooms, dining rooms, libraries, apartments and bedrooms also for the guests. Plasters, mural paintings, portraits, furnishings and furniture of various styles but of good Sicilian workmanship testify the different tastes of the end of the ninenteenth century.

The marvelous garden surrounding the Castle was enriched with statues, fountains, couches, neoclassic coffee-houses and a labyrinth in masonry.

Since 1982 the marvelous Castle of Donnafugata is of ownership of the Ragusa City Hall.

The Hall of the mirrors decorated with stuccoes in marble and papier-maché in the colors of white and gold, with bloom racemes is really marvelous. In the walls huge mirrors enrich the furniture. The curtains are original with the valances in gilded wood with crown motif. The floor is realized with plates of asphalt as it was use up to the last century in Ragusa and Modica.

RAGUSA - CASTELLO DI DONNAFUGATA - APPARTAMENTO DEL VESCOVO - CAMERA DA LETTO

Bishop's apartment consists in two rooms: the living room and the bedroom. This last is furnished with valuable furniture among which the nineteenth-century wooden bed with inlays in gilded bronze and a small writing desk in Luigi XVI style stands out.

CALTAGIRONE

Historical hints

Caltagirone has a very ancient history: placed in a strategic position for the control of the lowlands in Catania and Gela, it was already inhabited in the age of the Bronze. The prehistoric remains recovered in its territory are the witness of it. The inhabitants of Caltagirone were potters since the most ancient times, and that is confirmed by the recovery of an ancient furnace of the V or VI century B.C. and a siceliota crater (preserved in the Museum of the Ceramics), that represents a potter while working, under Athena's protection. Not by chance the name of the city, according to the interpretations that the researchers have given to the toponym, derived from the Arab "Qal'at al ghàrun", or "Hill of the vases". "Oppidum Saracenicum" (Saracen City), Caltagirone also after the 1061-1091 Norman conquest, remained an Arabic center and Moslem for a long time. Risen with a new Baroque style, after the catastrophic earthquake of 1693 that razed it to the ground, today it appears splendid in its decorums and superb in the art of the ceramics that makes it unique in Sicily. Of great beauty is the Staircase of St. Maria del Monte (photo on next page): on every raising of its 142 steps there is a different covering of polychromic majolica. In the photo down there is a balcony made in terracotta with floral motifs of the public garden.

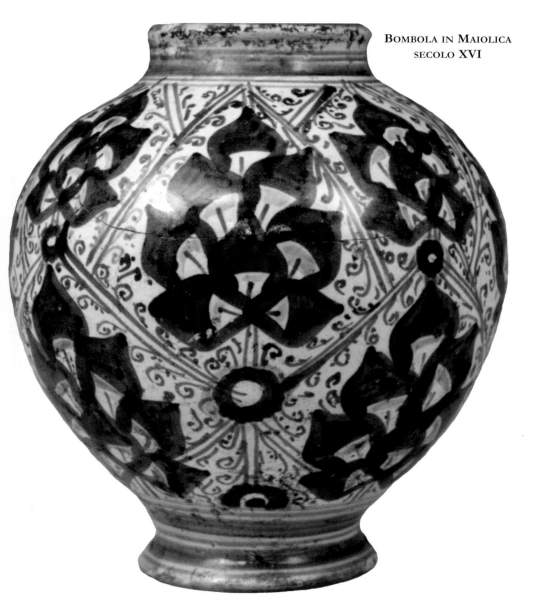

BOMBOLA IN MAIOLICA SECOLO XVI

CALTAGIRONE - THE REGIONAL CERAMICS MUSEUM

The Regional Ceramics Museum of Caltagirone was opened to the public in 1965 even if the collection of the majoliches of Caltagirone had already begun in 1948. Four huge rooms expose ceramics of various periods, from the prehistoric age to those of the 20th century, both of Caltagirone and of other places in Sicily. Those of prehistoric epoch handmade or made through manual lathe are among the most particular; the brown protomaioliches produced in the XIV century and the marvelous ceramics with blue ground, with polychromic decoration of floral motifs of the XVIII century are of great beauty.

PAG. 149: NATIVITÀ DI GIUSEPPE BONGIOVANNI - VACCARO DEL XIX SECOLO

PIAZZA ARMERINA

Historical hints

Piazza Armerina rises on the slopes of the Hill Armerino; such location determined the addition to the native one "Piazza" (the way the country was called up to 700), of "Armerina."

Already populated among VIII and VII century B.C., it was later colonized by the Romans, whose witness is widely testified, by the Byzantines and by the Arabs.

In 1061, the Norman Earl Roger triumphally entered the city and he was welcomed by the citizen with great enthusiasm. The Earl made gift to the citizens of the image of a Byzantine Madonna that today is still preserved in a silver tabernacle, in the greatest altar of the Cathedral.

In 1161 it was destroyed by William I, the Malo,who reconstructed it a few years later. The reconstructed city flourished again and it expanded from the urban point of view, thanks to the privileges that William gave it, until 1299 when it was besieged by the Angevins.

The growth of Piazza was consolidated during the '600: the architectural aspect of the city is, in fact, dominated by the Baroque style even if traces of medieval buildings, of the Gothic-siculian period and of that Renaissance are evident..

Among the different monuments of Piazza Armerina, what awakes greater interest is the"Roman Villa del Casale". Without doubt, it is the most important Roman monument in Sicily and it is protected by the Unesco.

The excavations, already undertaken at the end of 1800, had dug out some parts of the mosaic floor. In 1928, thanks to the archaeologist Paolo Orsi, the mosaic representing "The works of Ercole" was found out. Only in the fifties the whole plan of the building was noticed even if, some rooms have not been opened yet. The Villa, built during the IV century A.C., was the country residence of Massimiliano Erculeo's imperial family. In the XII century William I destroyed the village and the villa was submerged by slime and alluvial earth.

The architectural complex was variedly constituted by four decorated sectors with over 3500 square meters of polychrome mosaics pave, with various subjects. Among these the mosaics of the room "Trichora" with "The works of Ercole" are quoted; the great corridor over the peristyle where "Great Hunting" is represented; the winter lunch room with "Small Hunting"; the principal room of the apartment, on the right in the basilical hall, with "Arion on the dolphin"; the private hall of the Villa with the "Ten girls in bikini" and the gym of the vast thermal complex with the scene of the "Circus".

PIAZZA ARMERINA - VILLA DEL CASALE -"DIAETA" DELLA PICCOLA CACCIA

The mosaic represents one of the episodes of a small hunting beating all Villa del Casale's guests took part into. The scene shows two bloodhounds hunting a wolf.

PIAZZA ARMERINA - VILLA DEL CASALE - CUBICOLO DELLA SCENA EROTICA

The mosaic represents an erotic scene, in which a young woman lets herself be entertained by a crowned ephebe. It is the best preserved mosaic in the Villa del Casale.

PIAZZA ARMERINA - VILLA DEL CASALE - VESTIBOLO DI POLIFEMO

The great mosaic represents Polifemo receiving by Ulysses a full crater of wine. The scene fills the whole surface of the room .

MORGANTINA

Historical hints

Recovered at the beginning of the 20th-century, Morgantina was founded by the Greeks in the V century B.C. The city had probably developed on an ancient inhabited area of Morgeti, dating around 1000 B.C., but it reached its maximum development in Hellenistic and Roman age. Destroyed by Ducezio in 459, it was reconstructed in the second half of the IV century B.C., during the kingdom of Syracuse tyrant Agatocles, with whom it came to a great economic prosperity. Allied to the Carthaginians against the Romans, during the second Punic War, (214-211 a.Cs.), it was assigned for punishment to Hispani mercenaries, that determined with their occupation the definiti-

ve decadence around 100 B.C.. The excavations have dug out the remains of public buildings and of the Gymnasium, the theater, the macellum (shops), the barn, the furnace, the scalea of the Agorà, etc… At the center of the Agorà, the building structures of the sacred area have been considered as a Sanctuary of the V-III century B.C., devoted to the underground divinities. On the hill there is the residential district with refined residences, wall decorations and the illustrated floor mosaics (III century A.C.) like the one reproducing the myth of Ganymede, the cupbearer of the gods.

CASA DI GANIMEDE

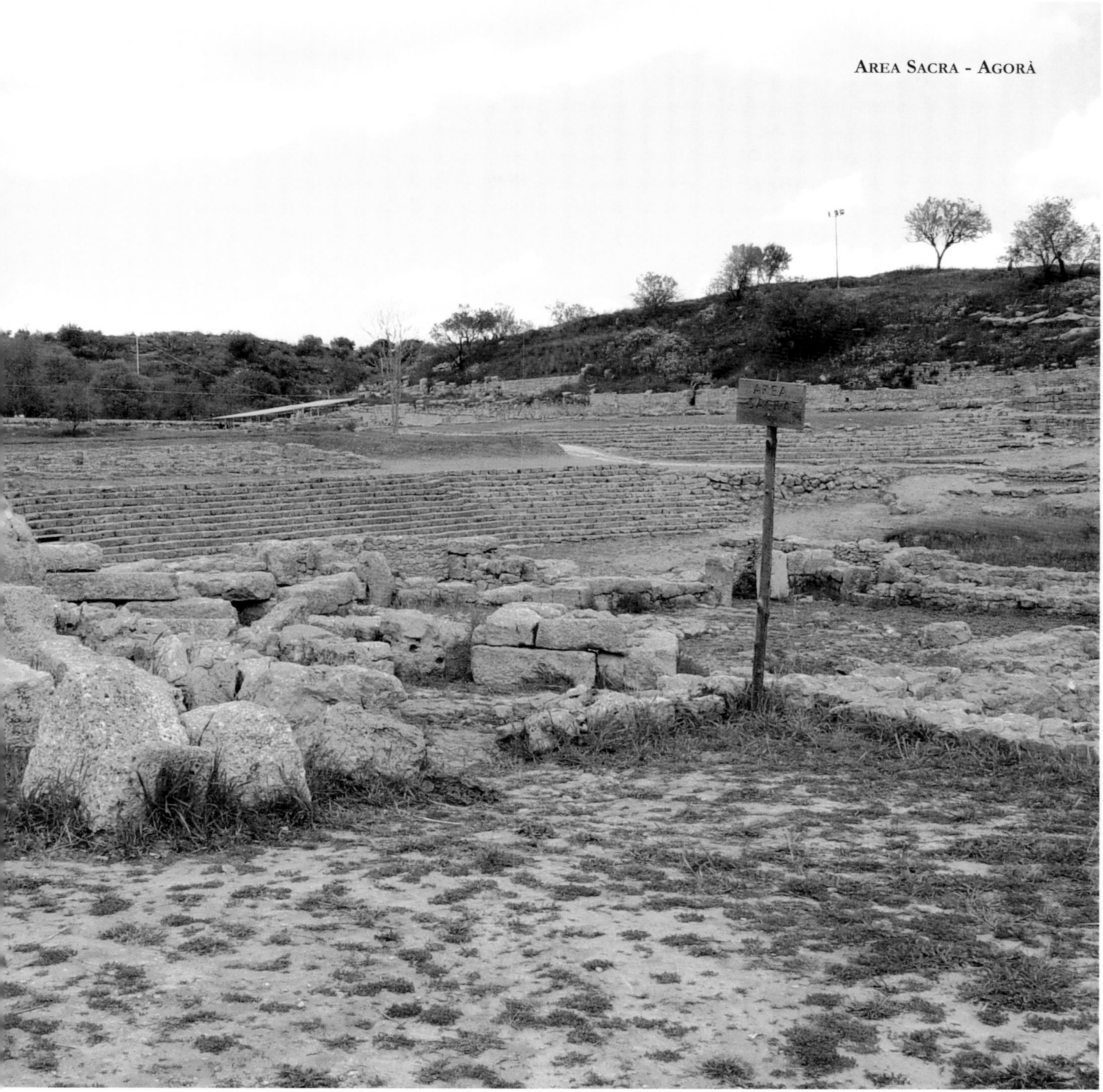

ENNA

Historical hints

Enna, the highest chief town of province in Italy, is said "Belvedere of Sicily". Founded by the Sicanis during the peace with the Siculians, it was conquered by the Greeks in the IV century B.C. The city saw a succession of different dominations: the Carthaginians conquered it in the 259 B.C. and the Romans freed it the next year. Under the Roman dominion the city developed the grain cultivations and its urbanism. The Byzantines chose it as strategic point of defense for its privileged position and in the 859 A. C. it was conquered by the Arabs that made it even more flourishing. The economic wealth already brought by the Arabs grew under the Normans (1087). Here Frederick II of Aragona assumed the title of king of Trinacria and summoned the first Sicilian Parliament. On a preexisting Arabic fortification, he had a Castle built in order to watch the valley and he used it as a personal residence. It still preserves six of the original Towers, one of which, the Torre Pisana, is perfectly preserved. The Castle, also called of Lombardy, probably for its closeness to a Lombard colony, founded in the Norman period, is among the most interesting best preserved medieval castles in Sicily.

ENNA - CASTELLO

ENNA - REGIONAL ARCHAEOLOGICAL MUSEUM "VARISANO"

The findings contained in the Regional Archaeological Museum "Varisano" of Enna, allow the reconstruction of ancient forms of life of the native people living in the territory of Enna, from the end of the III millennium B.C. to the Hellenistic-Roman age. The collections, coming from excavations, from acquisitions by private citizens or from Syracuse and Agrigento museums, are put in order following a topographical criterion of the origin sites. In the photo there are some terracotta statuettes of Hellenistic age coming from the territory of Enna.

SAN GIOVANNI BATTISTA

SAN GIOVANNI EVANGELISTA

ENNA - MUSEO ALESSI

The Museum Alessi takes the name from the clergyman Giuseppe Alessi from Enna who, at the end of the '700 and the beginning of the '800 gathered several archaeological findings and works of art. The Museum contains the Cathedral Treasure, among which its " Madonna's Crown" with enamels and precious stones; the Picture-gallery, the Archaeological section, the Numismatic section containing over two thousand Siculian-punic , Greek-siculian, Roman and Byzanthine coins, the section of Vestments and Church Ornaments. The poliptych representing St. Giovanni Battista and St. Giovanni Evangelista, dated 1594 is attributed to Antonello Crescenzo, called "The Panormita".

CALTANISSETTA

FONTANA DEL TRITONE

Historical hints

"Nissa", as Thucydides tells, in 427 B.C. was a small city of Sicily garrisoned by the Siracusanis. It became a Roman colony in 123 B.C., after having been annexed to the eastern empire, under Costantino, it was called Kastra-Nissa by the Saracens that conquered it. The city developed around the Saracen castle of Pietrarossa but in 1086 it was conquered by the Earl the Norman . With Roger the territory was reorganized and brought under the jurisdiction of the Latin Church. Dominated by the Swabians, the Angevins and by the Aragonites, it became a County during the kingdom of Pietro I of Aragon in 1282. From the XV century up to the '600, the county that had passed to Moncada's family of Paternò, expanded building new districts and roads. Charles V of Austria and in 1700 the Borbonis were Monacadas' successors.

Later the city went through a period of decadence that lasted until 1818 when it raised to chief town and in 1844 to diocese. The whole nineteenth-century period was important for Caltanissetta economics linked to the exploitation of sulphur mines. The competition of America put an end to this wealth and brought to the consequent closing of the mines that today are only a tourist attraction.

On Piazza Garibaldi, among the many monumental buildings there is the Cathedral entitled to St. Maria la Nova and St. Michael. The church was built between 1570 and 1622 in late-Renaissance style.On both sides of the façade two bell towers of 1840 stand; they are not of great scenographic effect but the inside is magnificient and of extraordinary beauty. The central nave is a galaxy of stuccoes and of frescos of the Flemish painter Guglielmo of Borremans who worked for it in 1720. The three central scenes that represent "The immaculate Conception", "The crowning of the Virgin" and "The Triumph of St. Michael", are enriched with puttos, clouds and in bloom shoots.

MUSSOMELI

Historical hints

Mussomeli rises at 750 meters above the level of the sea, on a plateau circumscribed by the river Platani and by the streams Belice, Salito and Tumarrano.

As many sites in the territory show, it seems the first settlement to date back to VI-IV millenniums B.C..

In 260 B.C. it was inhabited by the Romans and later by the Byzantines and by the Moslems in 831, therefore by the Swabians, Angevins and Aragonites The most significative part of the town which still shows all its splendour belongs to the fourteenth and fifteenth-century and was built on the remains of the castle that Manfredi III Chiaramonte had built.

As a manuscript of 1392 shows, King Martino ceased all the feuds to Guglielmo Raimondo Moncada, which already belonged to Manfredi III Chiaramonte and among these also "castrum Musumelis."

In Mussomeli dominion seven more dominions followed after the Chiaramontes: the Moncadas, the Pradeses, the Castellars (Catalans), the Perapertusas, the Ventimiglias, the Campos and the Lanzas. These last ones governed the country since 1549 to July 20th 1812, date in which the Sicilian Parliament in Palazzo dei Normanni in Palermo decreed the abolition of the feuds.

From the summit of a rock, in all its magnificience Castle of Mussomeli stately stands out. It was built by Manfredi III Chiaramonte between 1364 and 1370. Settled on hard stone, it still presents original elements in some rooms, as for example the groins that support the vaults of the rooms or the decorated capitals. Still well preserved, thanks to the restaurations done at the beginning of last century, there are many rooms and a chapel where the ruins of an altar and frescos of the XIV century are visible.

AGRIGENTO

Historical hints

It was founded by settlers of Gela of rodio-cretese origin in 582 B.C., but its certain origin goes back to the prehistoric epoch. Traces of the Greek presence on the place since the VII century also induce to consider a following and later foundation; the city was called "Akragas". Its expansion was rapid toward the hinterland and already under Terone (488-473 B.C.) its territory expanded to Himera, on the opposite bank of Sicily. Here the inhabitants of Agrigento, allied with the Siracusanis of the tyrant Hieron, fought with the Carthaginians, defeating them in 480 B.C. Its position and the supremacy on the island for the control of the maritime traffics, kept on causing rivalry with the Carthaginian so that in 406 B.C. the city was sacked and conquered by Hannibal and Imilcone. In 317-289 it was defeated by the Syracuse tyrant Agatocles. Allied to Carthago in 264 B.C., at the beginning of the first Punic War, it was conquered by the Romans in 261 B.C. and again during the second Punic War in 210 B.C.. The Romans called it Agrigentum and under their dominion it had great commercial and agricultural importance. In fact, in the II and III century

B.C. it lived in prosperity becoming a great emporium, especially with August. The commercial traffics with eastern countries and with the Italic cities led to a new wealth; the city and the defensive constructions were rebuilt, temples, public and private buildings restored. With the decadence of the Western Roman Empire, Agrigento suffered the invasions of the Vandals of Genserico (428-441 B.C.) and of the Byzantines in the 535 B.C. In 840 Moslems invaded the city that they called "Gergent" and they made it their settlement on the acropolis. Conquered by the Normans in 1086, it was also raised to Episcopalian center among the most important of the island. With the Chiaramontes in the XIV century A.C. it obtained the concession of the customs immunities in the maritime ports and this contributed to make its commerce prosperous.

The city gained its Roman name only in 1927, but the ancient Akragas remains as the unique area in the world showing a perfect blend of harmony between natural landscapes and marvelous ruins. This is the reason why it is considered "the most beautiful city of the mortals".

AGRIGENTO
TEMPIO DELLA CONCORDIA

The whole archaeological area in Agrigento has been declared "World Heritage Site" by the Unesco.

The Valle dei Templi represents the main place of Akragas sacred life. During the nineties years nine temples were erected in the doric order in sandstone tuff congiferopus, the local calcareous stone of yellow color. The remaining monuments belong to the V century B.C., the period of greatest prosperity for the city. Perfectly preserved and magnificent in its greatness, Tempio della Concordia is in the center of the Valle dei Templi. It was erected in the V century B.C. and it is a classical example of doric temple. We don't know exactly whom it was devoted to, but Tommaso Fazello (1498-1570) called it "Tempio della Concordia" from a Latin inscription found near the building. In the VII century A.C. it was changed by the bishop of Agrigento Gregorio in the Christian Basilica and devoted to SSs. Pietro and Paolo. Only in 1788 it returned to its primitive forms.

Erected between 460-440 B.C., just in front of the Tempio della Concordia, it dominates from the summit the whole Valle dei Templi. It was built according to the canons of the doric order, it was dedicated to Giunone Lacinia , gods' queen and Jupiter's wife.

In 406 B.C. it was set on fire by the Carthaginians and later restored by the Romans. Of the 34 original columns only 25 have been erected.

AGRIGENTO - TEMPIO DI HERACLE

Among all the temples in Agrigento, the most ancient is the one devoted to Hercules, Zeus's halfgod child , dating back to the end of VI century B.C. Of the original 38 columns only 8 are still raised.

It was devoted to Hercules, probably for Cicero's witnesses who told about it in a passage of the Verrine.

AGRIGENTO - TEMPIO DI GIOVE TELAMONE

The gigantic Telamone about m.7,75 tall beyond its decorative architectural function, sustained, together with the pillars and the half-columns, the heavy trabeation of the temple. Three Telamonis supporting three towers are figured in Agrigento armorial bearing.

AGRIGENTO - TEMPIO DI CASTORE E POLLUCE

In the sacred area there is the doric building, devoted to the Dioscuris or also called of Castore and Polluce, Zeus's twin children. The temple was raised in the V century B.C. Its four raised columns were reconstructed in the last century, precisely in 1836 by the architects Villareale and Cavallari.

"Lonely house in the middle of the native country… " So the writer, Luigi Pirandello, born in Agrigento in 1867, defined the house in which he was born. Nobel Prize for literature in 1934, Pirandello is considered one of the most important authors of fiction, essays and theatrical works of the Italian and European nineteenth century literarure. His house, declared national monument, contains today the Museum of the "pirandelliane memories".

VASE OF GELA

AGRIGENTO - MUSEO ARCHEOLOGICO REGIONALE

Inaugurated in 1967, the Museum contains findings of excavations originating both from Akragas and from prehistoric sites of the surrounding territory. The gathered material is disposed according to a chronological criterion; in the first room there is an archaeological plant showing ancient Akragas, useful to better understand its urbanistic development. The other halls contain the prehistoric findings of II and I millennium B.C., a collection of ceramics in black and red figures, findings coming from the Hellenistic-Roman district, silver, bronze and golden Greek, Roman, Byzantine and Norman coins, sculptures, a colossal Telamone of Zeus's Temple and three Telamons' heads.

PANTELLERIA

Historical hints

A paradise in the middle of the sea placed between Africa and Sicily, Pantelleria is the fourth island by extention. Of vulcanic origin it has a circular shape and from the top of Montagna Grande, in the middle of the island, during the clear days you can observe at the same time, both Sicilian and African beautiful coasts.

Signs of the ancient volcanic activity can still be found around the Montagna Grande crater, where 24 little craters are placed, called in the site "Cuddie".

Big steam drafts come out from the rocks clefts at the feet of the mountain and they plunge into the "Specchio di Venere", a little lake nourished from thermal springs that can reach the temperature of 50-Celsius degrees. In other places there are any outpouring of smoky steams called "favare" or "mufete".

The island presents splendid coasts and marvellous shores,needles,creeks,caves and particular rocks like the "cossirite", so called because of the island called from Greeks "Cossyra".

The first peoples living there and documented by signs date back to the Neolithic period and probably came from Tunisia.

As a witness of these presences there are still the "Sesi", Neolithic graves of 5000 years ago, with elliptic shape and many entrances, long corridors and cells of different sizes. In the Neolithic village, we still have traces of habitations and huts in which ceramics, majolica, obsidian objects, (the black volcanic stone), and various tools have been found. Round about the IX century the island was occupied by Phoenicians who remained until the second Punic War, when Romans arrived on 217 B.C.

After the fall of the Roman Empire it was dominated by Byzantines that enriched it with their splendid mosaics.

The Arabs that controlled it for 400 years named it Pantelleria and they called it "Bent-el-rion" that is " wind daughter". These cultivated vineyards and caper yards using the terracing system and delimiting the fields with little stonewalls.

Pantelleria has got a wide range of contrasting colours that get from the marvellous blue of the sea to the black of the rocks, from the green of cultivated countries, to the white of "dammusi", the characteristic white habitations. All this invites you to spend some days in it, enjoying all the wonders that only Sicily can offer.

LAMPEDUSA

Historical hints

Lampedusa, a paradise for scuba divers, is probably the wildest Sicilian island.With Linosa and the little island of Lampione, it makes the group of Pelagie Islands and it is 113 km far from the coasts of Tunisia.

The three islands, emerged from the sea depths, present different features: Lampedusa and Lampione have a calcareous origin, whereas Linosa is volcanic.

Lampedusa is the widest island of the archipelago and its name comes from The Greek-Byzantin "Lapodusa" that means "rich of molluscs".

Because of its geographic position, in the middle of the Mediterranean, it was a maritime post for many peoples like Phoenicians, Greeks, Romans and Arabs, as the found traces can testify. Many different Arabian, Turkish, Venetian, French, Maltese coins confirm it; but even more the Roman ones in the graves, near the "Grotta della Regina", that testify the Roman presence in the island, in the epoch of the Punic Wars.

In fact, Lampedusa and Linosa were used as a naval and strategic base for the expeditions against Carthago. After the banishment of Saracens from the island, in 813 a.C., we haven't had any news for about six centuries.

In 1430 Alionso V d'Aragona, first king of Naples, governed on it and gave Giovanni de Caro of Montechiaro's barons all the powers on the Lampedusa island. In the Byzantine period a combat carried out between Saracens and Byzantines and in 1551 the Genovese Admiral Andrea Doria, serving CarloV, during an expedition against the Turkish corsairs, led by their commander Dragut, was shipwrecked there.

Only in 1843 Ferdinand II of Borbone bought the island from the prince Tomasi di Lampedusa and issued an edict by which the subjects were invited to move in order to live there and cultivate it. After Garibaldi's expedition in 1860 the Pelagie Islands were annexed to the Italian Reign. It was even a site for a penal colony in 1872: in fact it was impossible for prisoners to escape from the island and they spent their time cultivating lands or helping fishers, with the obligation to come back in the evening at the trumpet sound.

During the Second World War it turned into a military fortress and suffered many bombardments by the Allies, in particular during the landing to Sicily.

Lampedusa is in great demand today thanks to its marvellous sea and its warm climax. Its fretted coasts, sheer from the Mediterranean Sea and its white shores are a priceless sight. Its big fleet is wholly taken with the sponge fishing and with the pesce azzurro (blue fish), stored in local factories.

It has been Natural Reserve since1995 for the protection of the "macchia mediterranea" and a port for many vegetal and animal species which are getting to the extinction, as the "Caretta-caretta" turtles that regularly deposit their eggs in the beach of Conigli.

SELINUNTE

Historical hints

Founded by the settlers of Megara Hyblea among 628 and the 651 B.C., Selinunte was the most western Greek colony in Sicily. Its name derives from Selinon, the river that today is called Modione and that flowed west of the ancient city. But the Selinon is also the wild parsley growing in abundance in the site of the settlement and as testified by the ancient coins of the mint of Selinunte, it was also the symbol of the city. Thanks to its geographical position, its splendid territory and the possibility of commercial exchanges with Africa, Selinunte was considered the pearl of the Mediterranean. The city lived in luxury and magnificence and the way of life was elevated. The tyranny of Teron of Selinunte, Milziade's son, increased its wealth, even not neglecting his work of government. At the beginning of the VI century the inhabitants of Selinunte began their colonizations occupying the southern coast next to Sciacca and they pushed on toward other territories in direction of Segesta, with which a long tension began ,that turned at the end into war.

In 409 B.C. the Carthaginians, after a siege of nine days razed it to the ground in one of the most terrible massacres of the ancient world. The greater part of the inhabitants were killed, the houses sacked and the dead bodies mutilates. The destruction of the city was completed at the end of the First Punic War, 241 B.C. by the Romans. The acropolis continued to be inhabited also in Christian-Byzantine and Arab epoch but in the Middle Ages we had no more news of Selinunte also because of a terrible earthquake that destroyed the few structures survived. The area of the ancient city was identified only in the middle of the XVI century thanks to the Dominican Tommaso Fazello, even if the excavations began in 1823. The archaeological park extends on a surface of 270 hectares, divided in the zone of the oriental temples, the acropolis and the sanctuary of the Melaphoros.

SELINUNTE
TEMPLE "C" OR
OF APOLLO

The bigger sacred building among those situated on the acropolis is the temple "C" or of Apollo, god of the oracles and prophecies. It was raised round about 560-540 B.C. and it consisted of 42 fluted columns. An earthquake destroyed the temple making contemporarily fall its columns and leaving them in perfect order. The temple was raised again among 1925 and 1927. A head of Medusa, that was certainly set in the tympanum, was found and preserved in the Archaeological Museum in Palermo, as well as metope, seals and cretule of clay.

SELINUNTE - TEMPLE "E" OR OF HERA

The Temple "E", realized round the 470-760 B.C., is a splendid example of Doric architecture. It is devoted to Hera, the Juno of the Romans and it is set up of 42 columns with sharp flute edge. Four metopes in marble belonged to this temple, representing female figures, preserved in the Archaeological Regional Museum in Palermo.

Mazara del Vallo

Historical hints

Mazara del Vallo is one of the best equipped ports of fishing boats in Italy and it rises to the mouth of the River Mazaro.

Its origins date back to the Superior Paleolithic, about 14000-12000 years B.C., and some natural shelters used by groups of hunters along the course of the River Mazaro, testify the presence of the first inhabitants in that place. In the Mesolithic period fishing was added the hunting and agriculture, especially lake fishing along the banks of the Gorghi Tondi, probably because of the abundance of fishes and fauna. About the Neolithic Age very little is known; while about the Copper Age (III millennium B.C.) near a coastal village, some graves dug in the rock which was entered through a cylindrical grit were found. Mazara was later and long contended by Elymians, Greeks and Phoenixes because of its strategic position. It was a Phoenician emporium and this is testified by Diodoro Siculo and it was confirmed thanks to the recovery, to the mouth of the river Mazaro and near Capo Granitola, of hundreds of silver coins produced by the mints in Agrigento, Catania, Gela, Imera, Leontinoi, Messina, Selinunte, Syracuse, Metaponto, Poseidonia, Sibari, Abdera, Aegina and Corinto. The Phoenicians called it "Mazar" that means "the fortress". During the First Punic War it was conquered by Romans and many remains witnesse that. Among the most remarkable remains there are three sarcophagus and an urn devoted to Cornelio Filone, preserved in the Cathedral and some remains of a noble building dated back to the III-V century A.C. with frescoed walls and mosaic floors. Conquered by the Arabs in the 827, Mazara lived a period of great splendour so that the Arabic geographer Edrisi defined it "splendid and sublime". The city became one of the most important district administrations of the island, that had been divided in "Val of Mazara, Val Demone and Val of Noto". Under the the Normans' dominion, in the second half of the XI century, the city became a bishopric and it was enriched with fortification walls with a Castle of which only a door has remained.

In 1862 to the name Mazara was added the term "del Vallo" to remind that the city had juridical-administrative power on one of the districts of Sicily, built by the Arabs.

Mazara del Vallo - Museum of the Dancing Satyr

Remained entangled in the nets of a fishing boat of Mazara, at a depth of about 500 meters in the channel of Sicily, in 1998, the statue of the "Dancing Satyr" was recovered, today preserved in the homonym Museum (ex church of St. Egidio). We don't know the exact date of its production even if for the position assumed by the young man, they thought to a typical scheme of the IV century B.C., but reproposed in the following centuries. It probably was part of a ship load that transported art works destined to the Roman markets of Sicily or peninsula. The lack of some pieces of the statue lets think that the depth can still preserve many other treasures.

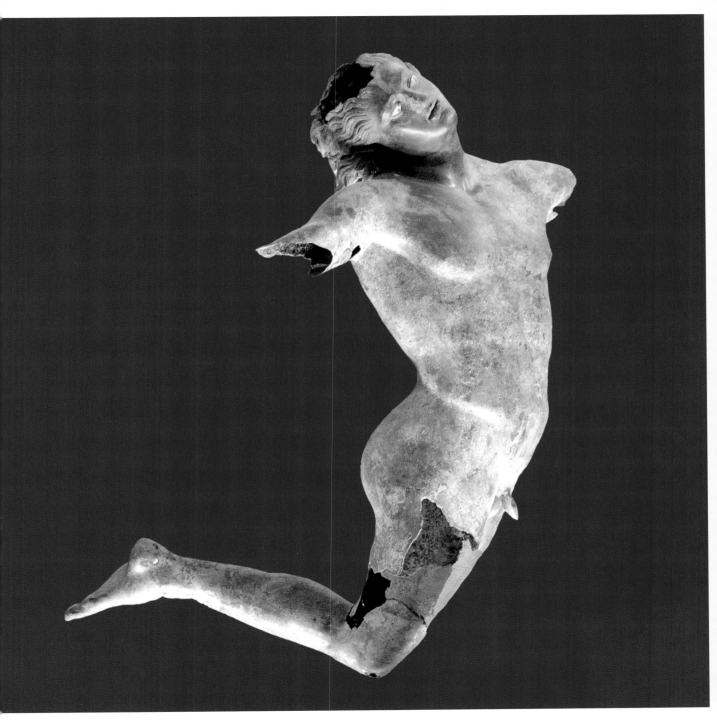

The Cathedral of the SS. Salvatore has been rebuilt in 1690 on a preexisting Norman construction of 1088-1093. On the portal a high-relief in marble manufatctured in the sixteenth-century probably represents the victory of the Earl Roger on the Moslem Mokarta; the eagle with open wings is the coat of arms of the Borbonis. Inside many works of art are preserved like a Christ Pantocrator, of the XIII century, a painted Cross, the Madonna del Soccorso by D. Gagini, the Ciborium, with the SSs. Giovanni Battista and Benedetto, the Transfiguration etc...

MAZARA DEL VALLO - CATHEDRAL OF THE SS. SALVATORE - "THE TRANSFIGURATION OF JESUS"

It is very interesting in the apse the marmoreal group of the "the Transfiguration of Jesus", sculpted in 1532 by Antonello Gagini and his son Antonino. The work consists in six statues of marble representing Jesus, the prophets Moses and Elias on the Tabor Mountain and the disciples Pietro, Giacomo and Giovanni.

MARSALA

Historical hints

Famous all over the world for its delicious dessert wine, Marsala rises on Capo Boeo, called once Lilybeo as the native name of the city founded by the Phoenicians. These ones in 397 B.C run away from Mozia, because of the destruction by the tyrant of Syracuse Dionisio II, the Old one and sheltered on the promontory of Lilybeo. There they united to the Elymians and the Sicans that already lived in that territory and they founded a new city that became point of coastal support for the traffics in the Mediterranean. Strengthened by thick walls and by a wide ditch, as Polibio and Diodoro testify, it became such an important Punic base in Sicily, to withstand, in 368-367 B.C., the attacks by the tyrant of Syracuse Dyonisus that was forced to withdraw. In 227 also Pyrrhus, king of the Epirus, that had come to Sicily to help the Siracusanis against the Carthaginians, after two months of siege withdrew. In 251 B.C. the Romans, engaged in the Punic Wars, conquered it besieging it through sea and earth. It became so the main naval base of the Mediterranean and port of connection with Africa. The city expanded and it enriched with monuments, houses and public buildings and was defined "civitas splendidissima". Conquered by the Arabs in the IX century the city was renamed Mars-Alì, Port of Ali or Marsa-Allah, Port of God, hence Marsala. The

Port continued to be the protagonist of the city that dealt with the most different goods with all the countries in the world. From the XII to the XIV century, under the Normans, the Angevins and the Aragonites, the city developed its medieval urban aspect: churches, convents, monasteries considerably enriched the city that increased even more its commercial importance under the Aragonese dynasty. The agricultural productions of wheat and sugar favoured the commercial exchanges, the military power developed and Marsala was rebuilt among 1600 and 1700 assuming its actual Renaissance-Baroque aspect.

At the end of 1700 Marsala developed the production of a sweet wine of high quality, that takes the name from the city, thanks to the Englishman John Woodhouse. During the IX century other families continued this production as the Ingham-Whitakers and the Florios that set up a series of factories giving start to one of the main industries of Sicily. On 11th May of 1860 Marsala was protagonist of Garibaldi's and his Thousand landing; Marsala, in fact, was selected by the hero for his glorious port, as his departure point for the conquest of the island and the reunification of Italy.

MARSALA - PORTA GARIBALDI

Garibaldi's landing, on May 11th 1860, represents an important date in the history of the unity of Italy and Sicily. Porta Garibaldi testifies the entry of the hero with his Thousand in the city. Previously called Porta di Mare ,the seventeenth-century door, surmounted by the imperial eagle, introduces in the historical center in Marsala.

Porta Garibaldi and Porta Nuova represent the two ancient entries that introduce in small roads full of churches, monuments, noble buildings, museums, picture galleries and theaters.

MARSALA
REGIONAL ARCHAEOLOGICAL
MUSEUM
"BAGLIO ANSELMI"
NAVE PUNICA

A part of the history of the ancient Lilybeo is contained in the Archaeological Museum in Marsala, located in the Baglio Anselmi today. The Museum contains witness and findings of the civilizations that have lived in its territory since the prehistoric centuries. The jewel of the Museum is represented by the "Punic Ship" of the III century B.C., found in the waters of the Natural Marine Reserve of the Egadi Islands in 1969. It is the unique exemplar of "liburna" found. The war boat is about 35 metres long, and it is provided with a range of 68 rowers settled in two sides. The evidence that the ship is Punic is given by the painted letters of the Phoenician alphabet on the prefabricated pieces of the ship, that lets think to a special technique of manufacture typical of the Phoenicians.

MOZIA

Historical hints

Among the low islands of the Stagnone lagoon, far a few hundred metres from Marsala, Mozia rises like a small splendid and verdant island that contains the remains of a Punic city destroyed in 397 B.C. and never rebuilt again.

Founded by the Phoenicians in the VIII century B.C. it economically developed thanks to the commercial exchanges that started in the Mediterranean, driving as far as Carthago on the African coasts. So Mozia became a Phoenician-Punic stronghold. It produced precious purple drawn from the "murex", a mollusc that was found in the waters of the island and used for dyeing the cloths. Hence in fact its name derives: Mozia means "spinning mill" and it seems that the city was really famous for the production of cloth dyed with the purple of the molluscs.

Helped by the Elimis of Segesta and by the Carthaginians, it defeated the Rodis and the Cnidis that tried to occupy Sicily. During the V century Mozia was center aspired by a lot of Sicilian cities until Dyonisus I, tyrant of Syracuse in 397 B.C. besieged the island using a new weapon, the catapult, and defeated the Punic fleet. Despite a long struggle, Mozia was defeated and razed to the ground while its survived inhabitants moved to the near Lilybeo, today Marsala. Later some families of well-off farmers returned to the island, but the city was not rebuilt anylonger; in the Middle Age it was called by the Basilian monks St. Pantalèo and only in 1906 the island was purchased by the Englishman Joseph Whitaker and took back its native name. Joseph Whitaker, very fond of archaeology, built a villa in Mozia, that today has become a museum, and he started an archaeological excavations campaign that dug out the Phoenician city. The most ancient finding is the archaic necropolis of the VIII-VII century B.C. in which have been recovered hundreds of cremation burials enriched with funeral outfits composed by majolica, weapons, jewels, etc... Next to the necropolis the tophet was found, a place of cult, devoted to Baal Hammon, in which children were sacrificed to the god. The Museum welcomes around 10000 findings among which a magnificent statue in marble of the second middle of the V century B.C. stands out representing the "Young Man of Mozia" and a sneering mask, maybe the first one to be recovered in Sicily.

MOZIA MUSEUM
YOUNG MAN OF MOZIA

MOZIA MUSEUM
SNEERING MASK

TRAPANI

Historical hints

Trapani is an ancient city of Sican origin called by the Greeks Drepanons, or scythe, perhaps because of the configuration of the promontory on which it rises.

Privileged for its position on the sea, it became an important emporium and a commercial port on the courses of the Mediterranean, getting more and more important in the VIII century B.C. under the Phoenicians. Under their dominion the Port of Trapani became an important naval base and strategic point of the Punic defensive system in Sicily. During the first Punic War it became a Carthaginian fortress and in 249 B.C. its waters were the theatre of the defeat of the Romans. Instead a few years later the Carthaginians were defeated by the Romans in the naval battle of the Egadis. Trapani, fallen into Romans' hands, remained like this till the invasion of the Vandals and later of the Byzantines. With the conquest by the Arabs in the IX century the city was rebuilt with a clear Islamic mark becoming one of the most prosperous cities in Sicily. Its splendour also continued with the Norman conquest, with the development of the commercial and sailor activities, and the handcraft workmanship of coral and gold. Giacomo II of Aragon in 1286 reclaimed lands and urbanized the coastal band creating new spaces. He built, besides, a small fortress called "Castle of earth". In 1500 Charles V continued the expansion of the city, the town walls were fortified and provided with massive bastions and isolated it from the dry land through the construction of a navigable channel.

Partly rebuilt after the 1940-43 bombardments, Trapani is today a modern city, with its port, that is the most important in western Sicily, its salt pans and its marvelous panoramas that space in the clear days up to the coasts of Africa.

TRAPANI - SALT PANS

Suggestive and spectacular appears to South of Trapani the characteristic landscape of the salt pans; an immense chessboard of rectangular tubs, used for the desiccation and the crystallization of the product. "The salt Street", so its itinerary is called, is dominated on the several islets of salt, covered by terracotta tiles, by the windmills, five of which recently restored, and by the low and lukewarm waters, place of standstill and nest-building for numerous kinds of birds.

The salt pans in Trapani are the most ancient but also the most active in Sicily; in Aragonese epoch they had great prosperity and the Arabic geographer Al-Edrisi had already described them in the XII century. Round about the end of the 800 the salt of the saltpans in Trapani was exported up to the northern Europe. For its organolepthic qualities still today this product is used and the saltpans are returning to the full activity. The saltpans in Trapani and Paceco are considered Natural Reserve for the excellent faunal and floral habitat that contains. Inside the Reserve has been a museum founded where there are all the ancient job tools, used for the salt working.

TRAPANI - PEPOLI MUSEUM

The fourteenth-century ex convent of Padri Carmelitani is now the seat of the Regional Museum "A. Pepoli" of Trapani. The building is adjacent to the Sanctuary of the SS. Annunziata, where the marmoreal statue of the "Madonna of Tindari" attributed to Nino Pisano is preserved.

The essential nucleus of the collections consists in Count Agostino Pepoli's private collections who was the founder of the institution at the beginning of the 20th century.

Together with the painting and sculpture collections, the museum illustrates the course of the figurative arts in the territory of Trapani, with particular reference to the applied arts in which the city of Trapani excelled, especially in the section of coral, majolica, gold, silver and sculpture dedicated to Nativity. Really the jewels, particularly the coral items, attract visitors' attention. In the past, in fact, fishermen, with boats provided of special talents, fished raw coral in the waters of Trapani to resell it to coral craftsmen. They refined in the time the techniques of workmanship and gave life to the flourishing artistic craftsmanship of Trapani that had its maximum splendour between the XVI and the XVIII century. Among the teachers of the XVI sec. Fra' Matteo Bavera stands out for its artistic gifts, of whom the Museum Pepoli has three works: a crucifix, a wine glass and a lamp, these last ones realized with the technique of the" retroincastro". A valuable saltcellar in coral, masterpiece of an unknown teacher, stands out among many domestic furnishings preserved in the museum.

TRAPANI - PEPOLI MUSEUM - CHALICE

The Chalice, realized with the technique of the "retroincastro", in copper, coral, enamels and silver, is one of the most precious works preserved in the museum. It is attributed to Fra' Matteo Bavera and it dates to the first half of the XVII century.

TRAPANI - PEPOLI MUSEUM "MADONNA WITH CHILD AND ANGELS REGGICORTINA"

Splendid in its colours, among the pictorial works contained in the Pepoli Museum, the painting realized to fat tempera stands out and represents "Madonna with Child and Angels reggicortina". A Valencian Teacher in the first half realized the painting, 108 x 77 cms.,in the XV century.

ERICE

Historical hints

The origins of this magnificent medieval village are very old .
Its birth is attributed to the Elymians even if the archaeological
findings on the Mountain St. Giulianos belong to   the
Paleolithic period and above all Neolithic one, that goes from
4000 to the I millennium B.C. A legend tells it was founded by
Erice, child of Venus, goddess of the beauty and love; to the
goddess, protectress of the sailors and revered by all the people
of the Mediterranean, called by the Romans "Venus Ericina", a
temple was devoted, in the V-IV century B.C., situated in the
place in which the Norman Castle rose.
In 510 the Spartan Dorieo tried to found a colony nearby but
the Carthaginians destroyed it. Among the 398-397 B.C. Erice
fell in possession of the Carthaginians and the Syracusans of
Dyonisus and during the Punic Wars the city was battlefield
among the Carthaginians and the Romans. The victory of the
Roman Lutezio Catulo upon the Carthaginians of Amilcares, in
241 B.C., put Erice in the hands of the winners. The city deca-
yed militarily also losing the defensive role on the
Mediterranean. Since then just a few news remind the city that,
passed under the the Arabs' dominion, changes even its name

in Ebel el-Hamid. The city flourished again during Normans's
dominion that gave it new splendour. Under the Aragonites it
had a good economic recovery, extended its territories and
resumed its role of strategic center of the zone. Also during the
Vespers war the population was faithful to its Aragonese rulers,
the city had different privileges and it was defined "Royal Earth
and Excelsa Civitas"
Between the XVI and the XVIII century Erice continued to
increase its economic comfort thanks to the flourishing agriculture and the profitable sheep-breeding. The building trade
developed also thanks to the activity of the monastic orders
and culture had a notable development with the contribution of
historians, literary men, clergymen and laymen.
Still now the town maintains its medieval features; it preserves
the cyclopic walls built by the Elymians around the VIII century B.C. on which traces of Phoenician inscription are visible,
the 1314 Cathedral in Gothic forms, the Norman Castle. The
visit in the city is an immersion in the past together with wonderful panoramas that space on the sea up to the Egadi Islands.

ERICE - CHURCH OF ST. GIOVANNI BATTISTA

Among the churches of Erice it is perhaps the most ancient, and it probably dates back to the XII century. It was rebuilt in 1430 in Gothic forms and reconstructed in 1631. Today, closed to the cult and used as an auditorium, it still preserves works of art of great merit as the marmoreal statues of St. Giovanni Battista and St. Giovanni Evangelista, realized by the Gagini in 1522 and in 1520, a stoup of the 1523 of gaginiana school and the statues of the Madonna of the XV century by an unknown author.

ERICE - CATHEDRAL

Devoted to the Virgin Assunta, the Cathedral of Erice was built in the XIV century by Frederick III of Aragon. Because of a ruinous collapse, among 1852 and 1862 it was restored and its aspect was modified. The inside, redone in the manner of the Neo-Gothic revival, preserves works of merit among which the statue of the Madonna Assunta by Domenico Gagini and another Madonna Assunta of 1523 by Giuliano Mancino. A stupendous marmoreal icon of gaginian school dominates the fund of the apse, realized by Giuliano Mancino in 1523, which represents "Madonna Assunta surrounded by the Saints Evangelists". Above there are bas-reliefs with scenes of the Christ's life. The external front shows a central rose window and it preserves the original Gothic forms. The bell tower, realized before the construction of the Cathedral, was used as a watchtower during the Vespers war in the last years of the XIII century.

ERICE - CASTLE

The Castle rises on the cliff in which the Sanctuary of Venus Ericina rose. From this one, in fact, the Norman building takes its name and this was built with the same materials of the temple. The fortress was the centre of the King and of the soldiers of the kingdom, because of the strategic importance of Erice. On the entrance door a headstone bearing the coat of arms of the Habsburgers of Spain is set. Inside the Castle we can still see the area in which the altar of the Sanctuary rose (thèmenos), remains of columns and fragments of friezes. The "Towers of the Balio" were rebuilt by the Earl Agostino Pepoli among 1875 and 1885.

Inside the habitation, typically medieval, you can admire the cyclopean walls built by the Elyimians round the VIII century B.C. but the several repairs made in Roman and Medieval Age have modified the original aspect. Along the boundaries several entrances are visible.
One of this is Porta Spada (VII-VI century B.C), Carmine (VIII-VI century B.C.), Trapani (VIII-VI century B.C); this last one has been rebuilt in the Medieval epoch.

CUSTONACI - LIVING MUSEUM CULTURAL ASSOCIATION

A few kilometers far from Custonaci, in a small village, called Scurati, made up of natural caves and houses disseminated as in a small crib, it is possible to visit in the summer period at the Museum of Arts and Crafts in the month of December, the living Crib.

The Museum, with the untiring cooperation of hundreds of people, in a fascinating ancient atmosphere, lets relive all the works that have characterized the life of our ancestors for hundreds years. During the visit, it is possible to taste some bread, ricotta, cheese and other things produced at the moment.

In the Christmas period, farmers, shepherds, women, children, sellers and animals, move in an atmosphere characterized by gestures, bawls, sounds and ancient scent making relive the mystery of the Nativity of our Lord Jesus Crhist.

Favignana

Historical hints

Western of Trapani, in the marvellous and uncontaminated Mediterranean Sea, the archipelago of Egadi Islands rises, made up of Marettimo, Levanzo e Favignana, which is the widest of the islands. It is made up of shelly and tuff calcareous rocks and in any caves, traces of a human settlement and a necropolis of the Superior Palaeolithic (age of stone) have been found, whereas in other ones, human remains of Mesolithic Age (9500-10000 B.C.). Besides there are remarkable signs of human presence dated back to the Bronze Age (1750-1400 b.C), graffiti and Punic inscriptions and ruins of the "Bagno delle Donne" of Roman epoch. The island got identified with the mythic Aegades, that is the Isola delle Capre told by Omero in the IX book of Odissey, to which Ulysses landed during the coming back to Ithaca. Phoenicians called it Katria, Greeks Aegusa, but in the Medieval Age it took its name from the wind Favonio, so it was called Favoniana. It was invaded by various peoples for several years, not last the pirates which forced the habitants to take refuge and living in the many caves of the island territory for a long time. The most ancient centre of the country was edified using tuff, the stone of Favignana that is still used as a building material in all Trapani countryside today. The island economy has been characterised by the tuna fishing for many centuries. To this activity the Florio family linked its economic prosperity in the second half of '800. The Tonnara Florio dominates the port and was built in XIX in order to work the tunas captured in the Favignana's tuna-fishing nets.

The whole island, in a big butterfly shape, reveals all its beauty in the low and fretted coasts and in its colours it charms for the transparency of its blue sea and its incredible bottom.

SEGESTA

Historical hints

Segesta is an ancient city founded by the Elymians, mysterious population settled in western Sicily. According to Thucydides, the Elymians were Trojan fugitives run away after the destruction of their city and landed along the coasts of Sicily. Here they united to the Sicans that already lived in the west of the island and assumed an own ethnographical identity. They adopted the Greek writing and also suffered the Aegean influence without losing their characterial independence.

The city had an important role among the Sicilian centers and in the basin of the Mediterranean and it was in conflict with Selinunte. For this reason it called in help the Athenians in 415 B.C. and immediately after the Carthaginians. The presence of the Carthaginians in Segesta drove Dyonisus, tyrant of Syracuse, to besiege it in 397 till it was destroyed by Agatocles in 307 B.C., giving it the name of Diceòpoli, or city of the justice. Later it took back its name, it allied, at the beginning of the first Punic War, with the Romans which in virtue of the common origin and Trojan descent for t Enea's stories, progenitor of the foundation in Rome, made it "libera et immunis" giving it a new development and great prosperity. They think that its end has occured because of the Vandals but, recent studies have revealed the presence of following occupations by the Moslems and Normans. Traces, in fact, of these presences are testified, in the acropolis north, where the theatre is, through the presence of a castle, a mosque and a church founded in 1442.

Of the ancient cities the elegant Doric temple and the perfectly preserved theatre remain, even if other witnesses are present on the slopes of the Monte Barbaro, constisting in ruins of a sanctuary in which two Doric temples dating to the VI and V century B.C. were inserted.

SEGESTA - THEATRE

The theatre, which opens in the background of the valleys resided by the ancient Elymians, is datable to the III century B.C.. Of semicircular shape, it has a great stairway divided in seven wedges. Its cavity, with the seats for the spectators, has a diameter of m. 63,60 and could contain up to 4000 spectators. Still now the theatre is stage of theatrical representations.

SEGESTA - TEMPLE

It is one of the most important examples of Doric style, probably built in the last thirty years of the V century B.C. by the Elymians, one of the first populations settled in Sicily. The temple has as characteristic the smooth not grooved columns; deprived of coverage and lacking of the cell, it lets think to an incomplete building, perhaps because of the conquest of the city in 409 B.C. by the Carthaginians, or to a construction destined to a cult under the open sky.

INDEX